Sex Magic, Tantra & Tarot

OTHER TITLES FROM THE ORIGINAL FALCON PRESS

Sex Magic, Tantra & Tarot

The Way of the Secret Lover

By
Christopher S. Hyatt, Ph.D.
&
Lon Milo DuQuette

Tarot Illustrations by David P. Wilson
based on designs by Lon Milo DuQuette

THE *Original* FALCON PRESS
TEMPE, ARIZONA, U.S.A.

International Standard Book Number: 978-1-935150-23-7
Library of Congress Catalog Card Number: 91-90459

First Edition 1991
Second Expanded & Revised Edition 1996
Third Printing 2004
Fourth Printing 2009

Cover by Linda Joyce Franks

The paper used in this publication meets the minimum requirements of the American National Standard for Permanence of Paper for Printed Library Materials Z39.48.-984

Address all inquiries to:
THE ORIGINAL FALCON PRESS
1753 East Broadway Road #101-277
Tempe, AZ 85282 U.S.A.

(or)
PO Box 3540
Silver Springs, NV 89429 U.S.A.

website: http://www.originalfalcon.com
email: info@originalfalcon.com

ACKNOWLEDGEMENTS

We express our thanks to David P. Wilson for
the execution of the Tarot trumps, Lon Milo DuQuette
for the conceptualization of the Tarot Trumps, and
Hymenaeus Beta for his version and use of The Tree of Life.

DEDICATION

MARSYAS
A.M.A.G.
SRI RAMADRISHNA
TO OUR SECRET LOVERS EVERYWHERE

TABLE OF CONTENTS

CHAPTER ONE

THE SECRET LOVER

Each of us has a Secret Lover; a lover who awaits just behind the erotic images that flood our minds during sexual arousal or in sleep; a dream lover who disguises as the individuals with whom we fall in love; an ideal lover who has adored us since the beginning of our individual existence and who will never abandon us until the instant we merge our being in absolute Godhead.

We momentarily feel the embrace of our Secret Lover in the ecstasy of orgasm and in moments of rapture when the beauty of music or dance or visual art or nature overcome us.

Whenever we experience a "broken heart" it is often because another individual has not lived up to the perfection of our Secret Lover. The reason sexual experiences are often better in the imagination or memory than in actuality is because it is in the imagination that the Secret Lover is nearest to us. Personal relationships will always be somewhat disappointing to us because in truth there can never be a relationship that matches the one we already have with our Secret Lover. It is the secret standard by which everything else is measured. The irony is that most of us are not aware of our relationship with our Secret Lover.

Surrender to this Secret Lover is a central theme of most every religion yet the doctrines and practices of the world's so-called "great religions" tend to dilute, deflect and deter the individual from the genuine personal experience.

Moreover the religious establishments have unceasingly striven to convince their congregations that this most private of all religious events is not a personal experience at all but an ambiguous and incomprehensible occurrence to be publicly affirmed and validated by the priestcraft. They, in turn, allow you to participate vicariously with them in a pantomime of the sacred marriage.

It is especially ironic that the mythical life of Christ exemplifies in word and deed the central secret of this divine relationship. Many passages of the New Testament and the newly discovered Gnostic texts clearly reveal that the Christ is a projected image of a *level of consciousness* achievable to all. And until this is experienced, until we have become one with *Him*, subsequent higher levels of consciousness will be unattainable.

Try as it might, the church has found it impossible to completely obscure this most sacred truth from the hearts of devoted individuals. The Ecstasies of the Nun Gertrude and St. Teresa are unmistakable examples of sexual surrender to the divine lover. It was only because of their religious and cultural environment that the image of their lover was that of Christ. Had Teresa been Hindu her lover may have been Krishna, Vishnu or any number of deities of devotion.

It is profoundly unfortunate that the forces of organized religion demand that, as prerequisite to uniting with the divine lover, the faithful must subscribe to the most ridiculous collection of dogmas and absurdities. Myths turned into lies, lies turned into laws and adherence to the laws has replaced the personal experience of the Myth.

Is it any wonder that the modern mind has rejected such spiritual self abuse? But isn't it sad that in doing so the "baby" of truth has been thrown out with the "bath-water" of primitive superstition.

The pages of history are red with the blood of illuminated "saints" who were murdered by their religions for actually achieving the advertised spiritual rewards.

In Western Hermeticism this Spiritual Lover is called the "Higher Genius," "Adonai" or the "Master Within." In the language of ceremonial magick it is called "The Holy Guardian Angel" and the union of the magician with this Spiritual Being is called the *Knowledge and Conversation of the Holy Guardian Angel*.

The *Knowledge and Conversation of the Holy Guardian Angel* is the primary goal of the ceremonial magician and must be achieved before any other meaningful magical acts can be accomplished. The Holy Guardian Angel (The Secret Lover) will be the magician's teacher, lover, mentor and guide through the higher levels of initiation.

Whether one considers oneself a ceremonial magician or not the fact remains that the above experience, no matter what it is called, is a prerequisite for complete spiritual liberation.

CHAPTER TWO

THE WILL TO SURRENDER
AND THE WILL TO SELF-MASTERY

*The will toward self mastery and the will to
surrender are the head and tail of the same snake.*

To surrender to love is one of the most misunderstood
experiences in human existence.

Intuitively we all know that to love and be loved is
both the spark and fuel of life. But how does a mortal
surrender to love when fear is so pervasive in our lives?
Without love life feels empty and meaningless. It is
unfortunate but true that most of life's misery is caused
by our inability to surrender to love. In a desperate
attempt to fill this void people become addicted to
alcohol, food, sex, endless affairs, fame, fortune and,
of course, drugs.

Frequently the use of love substitutes is not simply
an attempt to deaden pain but is also an attempt to
bridge the gap of separateness and join with the
Beloved. In Western Civilization the preoccupation
with these "substitutes" is "proof" that our society
doesn't really concern itself with love and surrender. In
fact much of Western psychology regards the desire to
unite with the Beloved as pathological. In the West,
love is simply licensed like a car.

SURRENDER IS NAUGHT

One of the primary obstacles to surrendering is the mistaken belief that you can actually "lose" yourself. This fear is based on a deep primal feeling that to love and be loved is a form of "cannibalism."

The desire to consume the love object and thereby merge with the beloved has been a romantic image that poets and lovers throughout ages have struggled with.

Though the boundaries of the individual must necessarily fade away there is no way in the world that you can lose your Self. Your true Self is *hard wired* in and even if it were possible to lose one's self or be possessed it would have to be the result of one's true will.

One real danger in love relationships is that most people secretly believe that they must control the love object in order to feel safe in loving and being loved. The cause of this is simple—children are made to feel that they must "give themselves up" if they are to be loved. Thus, for most humans the act of surrender has meant the loss of autonomy or worse—loss of one's own mind.

Surrender is neither control or morbid dependency and cannot be made contingent upon giving away one's "soul"; nonetheless, the person surrendering opens completely to the moment, and runs the risk of being deeply hurt. Sadly, in our society this is not uncommon and frequently serves to harden or embitter a person toward life in general. Or, on the other hand being deeply hurt in the act of surrender can lead to angry and painful "cries for help." When this occurs there is an insatiable and wrathful desire to be cared for as a child is cared for *and* the horrid fear of loss of independence.

Similar to the innate will for self mastery, the *will to surrender* has been exploited by religion, government and even the family. Far too frequently when little children surrender to their parents they are humiliated, shamed or even worse. When they become adults they, in turn, do the same to their children.

Radio and television are constantly attempting to exploit the desperate need for love. In their perverse forms of "entertainment" they create hysteria, foster the anti-life morality of collectivism and sell "pornography" as love.

They peddle their perverted ideas of romantic love and sexual union as ecstasy but their fiat currency cannot fill the hearts and loins of their viewers. The world still yearns for a love which few of us know. And this love is beyond anything any one individual can satisfy, yet at the same time this love can only be actualized through the love of another living person.

Much of psychopathology and many physical ailments are the result of the inability of the individual to surrender, to let go completely...to merge momentarily; be it with a person, divinity or one's own "secret lover." This is one purpose of this book, to help you discover your *will to surrender.*

Most so-called "sexual perversions" are abortive attempts at love and surrender. This is particularly true in "sadomasochistic" relationships where the inability to voluntarily surrender is dramatically "overcome." In fact many so-called pathological or perverse individuals are closer to understanding the true need for surrender and the willingness to experience it than those considered "normal" by society. The association of pain, bondage or brutality to love is not happenstancial. The facts are that in our culture love has been so intertwined with pain and loss that the so-called

17

"pathological" are often simply expressing the truth of how love really feels. They express a greater degree of honesty than the "average" person who in fact can express nothing about love and surrender.

Many murders and suicides have at their foundation the frustrated *will to surrender*. These violent acts are often attempts to be released from the hardened boundaries of one's private hell—to feel union with the "Other" or the Universe. The assassin of John Lennon is an example of a pathological attempt to merge with the beloved through the act of murder.

Most people feel unable to surrender or be in the presence of someone who is surrendering because of the pain it brings to the surface. They feel the pounding force of life pushing through their skin and they are horrified of losing what sense of autonomy they do have.

Often people who cannot surrender place themselves in situations which force defeat—a pseudo-surrender. Failure of this type is often "caused" by the person himself in a desperate attempt to consolidate diffuse feelings of anxiety.

In the afterglow of failure they allow themselves to indulge temporarily in an illusion of surrender. They can let go, but only in a sham fashion. This provides some sense of relief from the obsessive feeling of having to hold on to their tenuous sense of autonomy.

People who require strict bounds of individuality (guardedness) are usually the least capable of surrendering. Individuals firm within their autonomy are more capable of surrendering. This is identical to the notion that one must actually have a viable ego before one is qualified to lose it.

Those who have had their *primal sense of autonomy* severely impaired by an environment which stressed chronic self-defense to maintain their autonomy are all but incapable of surrender. Their sense of autonomy is so fragile, held together by pain and suspicion, that the idea of surrender brings forth intense feelings of shame, anxiety and guilt. Thus, they are incapable of giving love or receiving it. Their habitual defensive posture, learned when they were too vulnerable for differenti- ated defense, makes it next to impossible for them to drop their guard long enough for love to come in or for love to come out. Ironically, individuals such as these are often those who talk the most about love yet treat their relationships as an endless chain-reaction of nego- tiations centering around the issue of control.

The entire idea of "control," in this context, contra- dicts the result people believe "control" might yield— self-mastery. Here control means "control" of anxiety, smallness and the feeling of falling apart which an impaired sense of autonomy has created.

These fears and maneuvers are unfounded and unnecessary, once the person realizes that in reality they can only truly surrender to their Secret Lover. This act of surrender can do nothing but add to one's autonomy and power, but it is important to keep in mind that the benefits brought about by love are always a consequence, a result of surrender, and never the reason for surrendering. The need to surrender is "caused" by life fulfilling itself. Surrendering is a neces- sary experience for complete living and the *will to surrender* is the ultimate realization of this fact.

Giving love, being tender, showing compassion are as necessary as receiving them: none are a morality. They can not be legislated. They can not be enforced. They are a *result*, not a *cause*, of complete surrender.

MAGICK & MYSTICISM: A FALSE DIVISION

The concept of surrender has become so distorted that many believe that "surrendering" is in opposition to power, sex and self-mastery. This is one of the greatest lies.

Exposing this lie is another important point of this book—self-mastery *is not possible* without surrender. This issue can not be overemphasized. Magic and Mysticism—The Will To Self-Mastery and The Will To Surrender are two sides of the same coin. As it is often the case, pseudo Mystics see Magicians as power hungry individuals uninterested in love. These "mystics" see themselves in the service of love and humanity. In fact their attempt at superiority by appealing to those who can neither love or use power is proof of their lack of both. They are guilty of the greatest megalomaniacal maneuver—believing that they can love while all the time seeking esteem and power often by the most cowardly means. The "mystic" as described here has shrouded himself in the prophylactic of spiritual pride. You can almost rest assured that in his case—nothing will get in and nothing will get out. As people in the West are so suspicious of Magick little has to be said about the "false" Magician. He is already thought of as an egotist. Yet, it is the Magician more than the Mystic who knows that when power or love are taken to their extreme they become one.

Often this false distinction between magick and mysticism gives rise to strong prejudices against practices such as sex magick or the "Tantra of the Left Handed Path." These practices have bad reputations because they teach surrender *and* self-mastery. In other words, they teach love *and* power and not simply love *or* power. The idea of love *and* power is very disturbing to both those who require external controls to feel safe and to those who desire nothing more than to control others.

THE HEART OF THE MASTER

It is more than a colorful figure of speech to say that true surrender takes place in one's heart. The Anahata (Heart) Chakra of the Hindu system is traditionally opened in the act of divine surrender and the parallel experience in the Western tradition, the Knowledge and Conversation of the Holy Guardian Angel, is an experience of Tiphareth (the Qabalistic Sephirah corresponding to the heart Chakra).

It is from the Anahata Chakra, the "home" of the Secret Lover, that each individual finds their own true will and purpose in this life.

In order to know your true will, (to be the master) to "light up" with the divine, you must first surrender. The importance of knowing your true will is beautifully conveyed by Sufi Master Hazrat Inayat Khan:

> However unhappy a man may be, the moment he knows the purpose of his life a switch is turned and the light is on... If he has to strive after that purpose all his life, he does not mind so long as he knows what the purpose is. Ten such people have much greater power than a thousand people working from morning till evening not knowing the purpose of their life.

The power of surrender is divinely expressed by a description of one of the many samadhic experiences of the great mystic, Sri Ramakrishna:

> ...He explained that it was impossible to express in language the ecstasy of divine communion when the human soul loses itself in the contemplation of the

Deity. Then he looked at some of the faces around him and spoke at length on the indications of character by physiognomy. Every feature of the human face was expressive of some particular trait of character... And so the marvelous monologue went on until the Paramahansa began to speak of the Nirakara (formless Brahman)... He repeated the word Nirakara two or three times and then quietly passed into samadhi, as the diver slips into the fathomless deep.

...We intently watched Ramakrishna Paramahansa's samadhi. The whole body relaxed and then became slightly rigid. There was no twitching of the muscles or nerves, no movement of any limb... The lips were parted in a beatific and indescribable smile, disclosing the gleam of the white teeth. There was something in that wonderful smile which no photograph was ever able to reproduce... As the music swelled in volume the Paramahansa opened his eyes and looked around him as if he were in a strange place. The music stopped. The Paramahansa looked at us and asked. 'Who are these people?' Then he slapped the top of his head vigorously and cried: 'Go down, go down!'

Something similar to this happened to the famed Western Mage Israel Regardie. During the time that Dr. Regardie and Dr. Hyatt were putting the finishing touches on Regardie's *Complete Golden Dawn System of Magic*, (Falcon Press, 1985) he went to his usual chair and had a few cocktails. He excused himself and went to his room. We didn't hear a sound from him for an hour or more. Suddenly, we heard a shout, a yell in Hebrew; he was talking to his Holy Guardian Angel. We looked in on him; he was having a conversation with his Holy Guardian Angel, asking "him" to use him (Regardie) in anyway he saw fit just so long as "he" used him. Regardie was in an ecstatic state. He looked as if he had "left this world," almost angelic. A few moments later, he "awoke" and was told what had happened. He replied, in awe and amazement, "I have no memory of it. This is the first time that (it) ever happened to me that way." Later, he would say:

> This should happen more often to those in the Western Tradition, but they are too blocked, too much in the head. Instead of working, they talk too much ... too worried about attributions ... morality ... etc... without living them. (Laughter)

One way that we in the West can understand our ability (or inability) to achieve this type of surrender is by utilizing the archetypal images of our own psyche. The images of the Tarot have, for centuries, allowed the diligent seeker an opportunity to "eaves drop" on the pictorial language of the subconscious mind.

These images can also help us understand and formulate our *will to surrender* to the Secret Lover. We will explore the Tarot next before we continue with the search for our Secret Lover.

CHAPTER THREE

THE HOLY GUARDIAN ANGEL
AND THE ULTIMATE DIVINATION

Tarot authorities have long maintained that Tarot divination is best applied to questions of a mundane nature. "Does he or she love me?" "Will I get that new job?" What will be my fortune for the coming year?"

It has been argued that the Mercurial nature of the Tarot makes it easy for the querent to be deluded by wishful thinking. After all, wasn't Mercury the God of thieves and liars? Didn't he trick the Gods by telling them the truth with lies and then turn around and lie to them by telling the truth? Can we really trust this system to give us serious answers to life's most important questions?

Our answer is *yes*. But in order to receive such significant answers we must contact a spiritual intelligence of a profoundly higher order than those usually associated with Tarot divination. This "being" is far more important to us than any Goetic, Planetary or Elemental spirit for it is closer to us than our family, friends or lovers. It is an intelligence who knows us better than we *think* we know ourselves. And the primary purpose of this book is to help you contact your Secret Lover because it is only by doing so that you will ever be able to discover the answer to the greatest question of all. *"What is the true purpose of my life?"*

Obviously to receive the answer to such a profound question demands a greater effort and a higher level of sensitivity than it takes to simply visit a fortune teller. You must be prepared mentally, physically and psychically to recognize the answer when you see it. In this labor you have only yourself to work with. Natural abilities that are presently "sleeping" within you must be awakened, developed and then fine tuned.

You have most likely come to the conclusion that no one else can do this work for you otherwise you would not be reading this book. So if you are ready, roll up your sleeves, *"...for if ye take but one step in this Path, ye must arrive inevitably at the end thereof."*

SEEING BEHIND THE SCENES OF EXISTENCE

Let us start with your psychic development.

Exactly what are psychic powers? Simply put, psychic powers are the ability to look behind the obvious, to see an underlying reality. For example, looking at a computer or television screen provides you with no clue as to what is going on "behind the screen." Yet we all know that something is indeed going on. This "underlying reality" behind the obvious is as real as the picture and contains important and powerful information. It tells you about the secret workings of the device.

If you want to tap this inner information behind the screen you need to acquire technical knowledge or develop a program to make the data visible. You must acquire the tools to unlock your natural powers and allow you to know and understand your destiny and purpose in this life.

The obvious question arises as to whether everyone has the power to "look behind the screen." The answer is yes, but as no two people are exactly alike, each of us have different abilities and handicaps. These psychic handicaps act as filters that prevent us from seeing behind the screen. It is ironic to discover that we have erected and installed these filters ourselves. We have been taught from earliest childhood not to "see" and more importantly not to listen to our inner Lover.

There is, however, a silver lining to this act of psychic self-blinding. The fact that we have done it to ourselves means the filters are not "hard wired" in. If we can learn *not* to see or hear then we can also learn *how* to see and hear again. In fact, what most psychologists or psychiatrists call insanity may be, in some cases, simply a premature or uncontrolled lifting of the filters. Some individuals considered insane may be those who have simply had a vision or heard the voice of their Secret Lover and then told the wrong person about it.

Each culture, religion and society teaches us not to see or to pay attention to our psychic senses. In this way they can claim to see and hear for us.

THE GREATEST GIFTS ARE ALWAYS TABOO

The development of one's power has always been a taboo. This frightening fact is particularly true in Western cultures where a priestcraft has traditionally been regarded as the intermediary between man and his Gods. When you possess your own Psychic powers and knowledge of your Secret Lover, the need for intermediaries vanish. Thus, even today, there exists strong prohibitions against developing or using your own powers. This is particularly evident in the modern Evangelical Christian movement which maintains that all paranormal or psychic phenomena, other than those chronicled in the Bible, are of Satan and designed to lure the unfortunate seer to eternal torment. Vigilance for such infernal influences extends even to those individuals and groups which believe in personal freedom and the responsible use of personal power.

BLESSED TRAUMA

As a way to remove the filters and help us develop our powers the Universe has conspired to slap us out of our slumber. These "...thousand natural shocks that flesh is heir to..." are painful experiences that force us to *wake up*. Many of you who are reading this book right now are doing so because the gods have somehow shaken you awake from the sleep of the masses.

While these "shocks" are necessary and provide us with the impetus to explore ourselves further, without developmental tools and exercises we are likely to fall back to sleep again. The Tarot is one such tool consisting of powerful images which, when used properly, can wake you from the slumber of happenstance.

KNOW THYSELF

Simply stated, the Tarot is a set of seventy-eight images symbolizing archetypal forces, personalities and situations. Every conceivable situation, interaction and combination are available for study and contemplation. As Tarot images are pictorial and most often vividly colored, they pleasantly and painlessly stimulate the human psyche.

Many consider the Tarot to be the visual spiritual equivalent of an encyclopedia of man's collected knowledge. Some go so far as to say that if a person were locked away with nothing but the Tarot to study, every secret in the Universe would eventually be revealed.

In our view, the study of the Tarot, combined with ritualized preparation for divination, can yield profound insights into the Nature of Self and help us to initiate direct conversation and knowledge of our Secret Lover.

ORIGINS OF THE ANCIENT TAROT SYMBOLS

Many stories have evolved concerning the origins both in time and place of these ancient symbols. Some boldly claim that the Tarot was created simultaneous with the creation of the Universe. Others have maintained that the priests of Serapis in Alexandria Egypt synthesized their knowledge and mysteries in a picture book. This they used to overcome the language barrier that frustrated the many foreign students who came to them for initiation and instruction.

By tradition the Tarot is the picture *Book of Thoth*, the Egyptian God of wisdom who taught mankind language and writing. The Greeks worshipped Thoth as Hermes, the messenger of the Gods and to this day the Tarot and the related branches of Western mysticism are referred to as the "Hermetic Sciences." The Romans, in turn, transformed Hermes into the swift-footed, trickster Mercury, the messenger of the Gods.

The most colorful theories of the origin of the Tarot cannot be substantiated but there are two points most modern Tarot authorities agree upon:

1. The Tarot cards were introduced into Europe in the Middle Ages possibly by returning Crusaders, or the mysterious Knights Templar.

2. There seems to be a direct relationship with the branch of Hebrew mysticism known as *Qabalah*. The

details and the practical application of this relationship was, until the 19th century, transmitted orally and protected from the profane by oaths of strictest secrecy.

But regardless of what is true about the origin of the Tarot symbols, the fact remains that they are powerful psychic stimulants that if used properly awaken the psyche and allow the Secret Lover to direct us in finding our True Will.

I have been a student of the Tarot since 1964, when at the age of twenty one I met an elderly lady who introduced me to it.

She had come to apply for the job of baby-sitter for my new born son Michael. After a few weeks she took me into her confidence and showed me her personal Tarot deck. It was hand painted with brilliant colors and was a bit larger than the store-bought model which she also showed me. She gave me lessons in the Tarot and then suddenly one day disappeared never to be seen by me again.

Since that time I have found that the Tarot, if used correctly and with great respect, can help remove the filters of the mind and help awaken us to the Secret Lover within.

This can be accomplished by performing a special divinatory procedure. The Ultimate Divination requires the same level of skill and preparation as an athlete who is preparing for a championship game.

Therefore, we highly recommend that you study what follows carefully, even if you already know a great deal about the Tarot and Divination. Some of the symbols derived from the Ultimate Divination will later be used in helping you contact and communicate with your Secret Lover.

CHAPTER FOUR

THE DANCE OF EVOLUTION: DNA-HGA

Each of us is a bio-electro-magnetic energy field. Our whole being is in unceasing joyous motion of DNA perfecting and experiencing itself. We move in a constant psycho-physical-spiritual dance of evolution.

Unfortunately the majority of us are completely unaware of this dynamic and evolving nature and so cannot begin to understand our true purpose in life.

Again, if we are self-aware enough to make excuses, we can blame influences within our culture and those who would enslave us for making us unaware of our own Karmic importance. But once we have begun to awaken to our potentiality we have no one but ourselves to blame if we allow ourselves to be "put to sleep" again.

The Universe is incomplete and everything in it is imperfect and in a dynamic process of completion. Each unit of existence (whether you and I consider it a "living" entity or not) is an organ of a unified Body of energy. As such, each organ has its own evolutionary history and is an integral part of both the past, present and future.

If we could identify with the evolving DNA of the Universe, instead of seeing ourselves from the point of view of our Egos, our names, our professions, we would have a far more accurate understanding of what Karma really is. We are active, growing, organic participants in the Body of the Universe not simply character actors in a morality play of our "personal" ego.

Whether we are aware of it or not each of us is already tuned to specific energy bands or frequencies of the One Life. Once we learn to fine-tune ourselves and harmonize our personal frequencies with the universal frequencies we come into direct awareness of our contact with the rest of the cosmos. A good example is that of a tuning fork that, once struck and set to vibrating can cause other tuning forks of like notes, even many octaves apart, to start vibrating. The universe is vibrating just fine. But our "tuning forks" are covered with so much "rust" (that has built up over countless generations of unemployment), that our sympathetic vibrations are at best muffled echoes.

Many people are unhappy and depressed because life seems empty and meaningless. They fear that they are not serving any purpose beyond some gross abstraction or biological necessity. They refuse to allow themselves to become mad and thereby insure that madness of the most mediocre variety will manifest.

Realization of the need to know what part we are playing in the Evolution of the Divine Body can occur anytime during one's life. In fact it can occur many times, but it surfaces most often during the latter half of life as we free ourselves from both biological and cultural imperatives.

Even then, most people satisfy themselves with the explanation their family, culture and religion provide as to their true will and purpose in life. However, there are others who require a deeper and more significant understanding and eventually realize that the answers must come from themselves.

For these individuals this book provides a means of knowing and understanding your relationship with your Secret Lover. By having this information at hand the serious student of life can begin to take a more active and conscious part in his/her evolution.

YOUR TAROT SYMBOLS

Your personal Tarot symbols represent the karmic momentum and tendencies you were born with and must contend with from birth throughout your lifetime. It is of primary importance to work with these symbols first as they serve to define you and pinpoint your relative position in the grand scheme of things. They will set the stage for what is to come and enable you to ask the question, "Now that I know who I am, what do I want to be?"

As in casting an astrological horoscope, your personal Tarot symbols are determined by your birth-date and can, if analyzed further, be amended and modified by the date of conception. But for our purposes we will concentrate on the birth-date as it represents your entry upon the time-space stage and your *initiation* as a unique character actor in this particular cosmic drama.

Unlike an astrological chart however, the Tarot symbols of your birth are pictorial and thus have a far greater impact on your conscious and unconscious mind. For example, no matter how many essays and criticisms you may read detailing the attributes of the Mona Lisa nothing could provide you with the same subjective, spiritual experience as simply looking at the painting itself.

It is no accident that the individual cards of the Tarot are referred to as "Keys" for that is exactly what they are. Even the most superficial meditation upon the symbols has been known to trigger significant changes in dream patterns and powers of imagination and concentration. Tarot symbols serve the purpose of stimulating your personal psychic powers and allow your conscious personality to become directly involved with your Karmic-growth.

CHAPTER FIVE

THE FOUR DIVISIONS OF THE TAROT

To help you understand the following information we ask that you take out your deck of Tarot cards and divide them as follows:

I
THE MAJOR ARCANA
CONSISTING OF 22 CARDS

Four cards that represent Elements:

The Fool (Air)
The Hanged Man (Water)
Judgment (Fire)
The World (Earth*)*

Seven cards that represent Planets:

The Magician (Mercury)
The High Priestess (Moon)
The Empress (Venus)
The Wheel of Fortune (Jupiter)
The Tower (Mars)
The Sun (Sun)
The World (Saturn)[1]

---

[1]No, you didn't add wrong. Planet **Saturn** and Element **Earth** are both represented by the same card, **The World.**

Twelve cards that represent
the Signs of the Zodiac:

Emperor (Aries)	*Justice* (Libra)
Hierophant (Taurus)	*Death* (Scorpio)
Lovers (Gemini)	*Art* (Sagittarius)
Chariot (Cancer)	*Devil* (Capricorn)
Strength (Leo)	*Star* (Aquarius)
Hermit (Virgo)	*Moon* (Pisces)

II
THE COURT CARDS
CONSISTING OF 16 CARDS:

These are the *King, Queen, Prince* and *Princess* of each of the four Elemental suits:

WANDS, CUPS, SWORDS AND DISKS

Fire	Water
King of Wands	King of Cups
Queen of Wands	Queen of Cups
Prince of Wands	Prince of Cups
Princess of Wands	Princess of Cups
Air	Earth
King of Swords	King of Disks
Queen of Swords	Queen of Disks
Prince of Swords	Prince of Disks
Princess of Swords	Princess of Disks

III
THE ACES
CONSISTING OF 4 CARDS

These represent the Primal Root of each of the four Elements; not the Elements themselves but the "seed" of each Element.

Ace of Wands, the Root of Fire
Ace of Cups, the Root of Water
Ace of Swords, the Root of Air
Ace of Disks, the Root of Earth

IV
THE SMALL CARDS
OF THE MINOR ARCANA
CONSISTING OF 36 CARDS

These are the small cards (2 through 10) of each of the Four Suits:

2 through 10 of Wands
2 through 10 of Cups
2 through 10 of Swords
2 through 10 of Disks

The total number of symbols are 78.

When we have completed explaining the process of determining your own symbols you will have:

1 card from the *Major Arcana*
1 card from the *Court Cards*
1 card from the *Aces*
1 card from the *Minor Arcana*
plus 2 very important support cards.

These cards are pictorial representations of your own personal qualities and powers and will be used in helping obtain the Knowledge and Conversation of your Secret Lover. It is essential however, before we start using the cards, to have a basic understanding of the exquisite system of spiritual exploration which the Tarot visually illustrates. This system is the Qabalah.

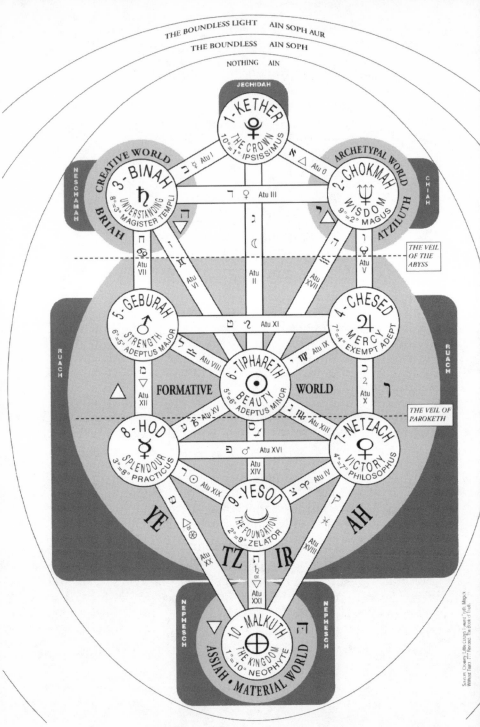

עץ חיים　THE TREE OF LIFE

The Three Veils of the Negative • The Ten Sephiroth with their Numbers, Names, Planets, Titles and Grades
The Veils of the Abyss and of Paroketh • The 22 Paths with their Tarot, Elemental, Planetary, Zodiacal and Hebrew correspondences
The Fivefold Constitution of Mankind • The Tetragrammaton in the Four Worlds

CHAPTER SIX

THE QABALAH, THE TREE OF LIFE
AND THE TAROT

Know first that the branch of Hebrew mysticism known as the Qabalah has, by tradition, existed since pre-historic times—and that there continues to this day groups of devout, Jewish scholar-mystics who have dedicated their lives to the study of the Scriptures and the "Qabalistic" interpretation of the same.

These Qabalists have very little interest in (or respect for) the Western Magical or Hermetic applications of Qabalah that developed during the Italian Renaissance and crystallized magnificently in the latter half of the Nineteenth Century in the teachings of the Hermetic Order of the Golden Dawn. With all due respect to our orthodox Qabalistic brothers, it is this "Western" system we are referring to when we use the word Qabalah and which we shall now briefly examine.

In Hebrew the word Qabalah (spelled QBL) means "to receive" and "to accept." Tradition holds that God taught the secrets of the Qabalah to the Angels and the Angels taught it to Adam. Adam therefore "received" the secret knowledge directly from Divine sources. It is amusing to note that QBL also means "to complain" and "to cry out" which any beginning student of the Qabalah will tell you is ripe with meaning.

A primary concern of the Qabalah is numbers. Numbers are used as symbols of abstract universal principals. One cannot watch a presentation of new discoveries in physics or astronomy without being "talked to" in numbers. A modern lecture in either of these subjects is patently metaphysical and delightfully inspiring to the Qabalist who sees each new astronomical development as a confirmation of basic Qabalistic cosmology.

It is not the purpose of this book to elucidate endlessly upon the Qabalah. (And it is not an exaggeration to say that *one could elucidate endlessly!*) We hope only to show the basic Qabalistic principals that are the foundation of the Tarot. To do this we will use the Tarot itself as our model.

THE 22 TRUMPS
THE MAJOR ARCANA
THE HEBREW ALPHABET

There are 22 letters in the Hebrew alphabet. Even the exoteric traditions of Judaism maintain that the Hebrew alphabet is more that just an alphabet of a Semitic language. It is, by tradition, the primary tool of creation itself. By uttering "words" made from these holy letters, God created everything in the universe. When God said ARTz (Earth) the Earth was created, etc.

(Note: It is not necessary to learn the Hebrew language to begin your study of the Qabalah. However, if you wish to embark on a more in-depth study of the Qabalah or the Tarot it is necessary to be familiar with the Hebrew alphabet and the various attributes of each letter. Please also remember that words in Hebrew are written from right to left.)

In perhaps the single most important Qabalistic text, *Sepher Yetzirah* (*The Book of Formation*), the twenty-two letters of the Hebrew alphabet are divided into three categories:

Three Mother Letters:

א מ שׁ

(A.M.Sh.)
representing the elements of
Air, Water and **Fire**

Seven Double Letters:

ב ג ד כ פ ר ת

(B.G.D.K.P.R.Th)
representing the 7 planets of the ancient world
Mercury, Luna, Venus, Jupiter Mars, Sol and **Saturn**

Twelve Single Letters:

ה ו ז ח ט י ל נ ס ע צ ק

(H.V.Z.Ch.T.Y.L.N.S.O.Tz.Q.)
representing the 12 signs of the Zodiac,
Aries, Taurus, Gemini, Cancer, Leo, Virgo, Libra, Scorpio, Sagittarius, Capricorn Aquarius and **Pisces**

It is easy to see that the division and correspondences of the 22 Trumps of the Major Arcana of the Tarot are identical to that of the Hebrew Alphabet. Both are positioned on the diagram called The Tree of Life which we will discuss later. (See diagram above.)

THE FOUR SUITS AND THE COURT CARDS
(THE FOUR QABALISTIC WORLDS)

י ה ו ה

(Y H V H)
THE ORIGINAL FOUR LETTER WORD

After the 22 cards of the Major Arcana the next most obvious characteristic of the Tarot is that the remaining 56 cards are divided into four suits; Wands, Cups, Swords and Disks which, as we know (or will soon find out), correspond to the elements Fire, Water, Air and Earth respectively. But why four? Why not five (to include Spirit?) or 3 (to match the three Mother letters?) The answer is found in the letters:

י ה ו ה

YHVH, pronounced *Jehovah* by the ignorant, a name of God so sacred to Judaism that to this day Jews are forbidden to pronounce it and instead, when they see it in print, replace it with the word *Adonai*.

This Divine name is called the Tetragrammaton and the four letters represent the totality of the forces and energies of creation divided into four distinct "worlds."

י

Y (Yod)

Represents the highest Spiritual Realm from which all other worlds are born. One could almost describe it as the Will (Wand) of God. This World is called *Atziluth* and is designated the *Archetypal World*.

ה
H (Heh)

Represents the *Creative World* where the archetypes of creation (coming down from Atziluth) are impressed into concepts. This World is called *Briah* and could be considered the Soul (Cup) of God.

ו
V (Vau)

Represents the *Formative World* where the concepts coming down from Briah are actually formulated into the "blueprints" of what will eventually become the material universe. This World is called *Yetzirah* and could be viewed as the Divine engineering department, the Mind (Sword) of God.

ה
H (Heh, *final*)

Represents the *Material World*—the phenomenal universe and all the energies, seen and unseen, that comprise it. This World is called *Assiah*. What started as the impulse of Atziluth became the concept of Briah that became the "blueprint" of Yetzirah, finally manifests in the fourth world, Assiah (Disk).

These four worlds are represented in the Tarot as the four suits;

> **Yod** represents *Wands,* the suit of Fire.
> **Heh** represents *Cups,* the suit of Water.
> **Vau** represents *Swords,* the suit of Air.
> **Heh** (f) represents *Disks,* the suit of Earth.

43

YHVH and the qualities of the Four Worlds also manifest in the Court Cards of the Tarot in a most remarkable way.

Each of the four suits of the Tarot has King, Queen, Prince and Princess of its own and their influence permeates the entire deck and the entire Tree of Life.

יַ **Yod** is the Father, a *King*. He "weds"

ה **Heh,** the Mother his *Queen*
   who gives birth to twins, a boy, and a girl;

ו **Vau,** the *Prince* and

ה **Heh** (f), the *Princess*

It is easy to see in the above "family story" the mechanics of the descent of Spirit into Matter. The Primal Fire impregnates itself upon Primal Water which becomes the womb for Primal Air and eventually the Primal Earth of the material world.

In the poetic imagery of the Qabalah, humanity is the final **Heh**. Like an enchanted Princess in a fairytale, we find ourselves trapped in the material universe far away from our Mother the Queen and our Father the King. Unless we are rescued we will never attain our rightful place on the Throne.

But rescue is *in the cards* for the story does not end here. This Court Card family is also the key to our *return* from the material world to that of the Divine.

ה **Heh** (f)   The *Princess* surrenders herself as lover to

ו **Vau**   The *Prince* who weds her. She becomes pregnant making her

ה **Heh**   the *Queen,* making the Prince

יַ **Yod**   the *King*.

The remarkable thing about these two stories is that they are happening eternally at the same time. Just as an alternating current of electricity passes through a wire in both directions simultaneously so too does the "electro-magnetic" power of **YHVH** pass through every level of creation including you and me.

We have already seen that each of us is the final **Heh**, the Princess living in Assiah far from our original estate. But who is this **Vau**, the Prince to whom we must surrender and who will be our Secret Lover and champion? Where do we seek the Prince? In the Western Hermetic Tradition he is called *The Holy Guardian Angel* and "he" is closer to us than our own heart-beat. He is our Secret Lover.

Knowledge and Conversation of The Holy Guardian Angel (The Secret Lover) is the Primary Spiritual Experience. Most religions and cultures speak of a comparable event.

The Royal Mass of the Secret Lover (see Chapter Eleven) is a Western Tantric ritual celebration in which the Holy Guardian Angel (in many texts, simply called 'H.G.A.') of each partner is invoked during sexual union. The two celebrants and their two Holy Guardian Angel's then literally become: ה ו ה י.

THE ACES
SMALL CARDS
THE 10 SEPHIROTH OF THE TREE OF LIFE

You will notice that the Tree of Life consists of 10 circles joined by 22 lines. The circles, called Sephiroth or Emanations, are arranged in three triangles with one Sephirah (the singular form of Sephiroth) hanging like a pendant at the bottom. It is important that you are familiar with this diagram as it will play an important part in your Ultimate Divination and invocation of your Secret Lover.

"God is One." This tired slogan of the world's monotheistic religions is nevertheless just about the highest thing that our minds can attempt to comprehend. We can't really grasp the concept of the Monad, (a singularity beyond which there is nothing), but we *can* think about *thinking* about it and that is doing pretty well.

If we could imagine *THE ONE* it would, naturally, be the thing from which all other *things* emanate, but what *other things* are we talking about if "All is One"? The appearance of the *many* must be just that—appearance—illusion.

If all is One then what is all this other stuff doing here and, more importantly, why do I feel so separated from *THE ONE*? These are precisely the kinds of questions that Qabalistic meditations tackle.

For the moment let us view *THE ONE* as the ACES of the Tarot and put all four of them in the top Sephirah position on the Tree of Life.

Because we know "All is One" we could stop right here in our contemplation of the universe. But that would not begin to answer our questions about where the *many* came from or how we are to surrender *to* and *with THE ONE*.

To think about these things we have to try to put ourselves in the place of *THE ONE*. What would it be like being *THE ONE*? Lonely I would imagine. I know that if I were *THE ONE* I would like to know who or what I was. This would be difficult because there would be nothing to compare myself to—nothing outside myself—no mirror in which I could reflect myself. The only place for me to look would be inside myself. So, like a good Yogi, I would sit down, close my eyes and in meditation reach deep into myself until I hit dead center. There at the very focal point of my being I would see myself reflected. At that instant the concept of *TWO* is born (1. Me and 2. My Reflection). Then simultaneous to the creation of *TWO* would occur the creation of *THREE* (1. Myself, 2. My Reflection and 3. The *Understanding* of the difference.)

This is how *THE ONE* became *THREE* and the reason why the Trinity is universally used as the ultimate expression of perfect Unity.

Now put all four number Two Cards on the Second Sephirah of your Tree of Life and all four Three Cards on the Third Sephirah

Again, we might just stop here and consider *THE ONE* in its three aspects, but we can't. It is already too late. The process of the creation of the *many* is rolling like a juggernaut with unstoppable momentum.

The same process that caused *TWO* to be created from *THE ONE* now makes the entire Trinity (One, Two and Three) reflect itself in a Second Trinity (Four Five and Six). And the same law that made the original *THREE* from the union of *TWO* and *ONE* now creates a Third Trinity (of Seven, Eight and Nine).

Put all four Four Cards on the Fourth Sephirah, all four Five Cards on the Fifth Sephirah and all four Six Cards on the Sixth Sephirah. Put your four Sevens, Eights and Nines on their respective Sephiroth as well.

Finally the whole process seems to make an attempt to start over again (albeit on a very low plane) and a tenth Sephirah is created which, in a very real way, reflects the original *ONE*. It is in this Tenth and last Sephirah we find ourselves and our material world. Some find it a bit depressing to think that we are so low on the Tree of Life. But take heart, isn't it good to know that we have such a good road map back.

Now put all four tens on the tenth Sephirah.

We will mention here that between the First and the Second Trinities lies the Abyss, an "area" of profound obscurity and mystery. After the magician has experienced the Knowledge and Conversation of the Holy Guardian Angel (which takes place in the 6th Sephirah, Tiphareth) the next great spiritual goal is the Crossing of the Abyss (passing from the 4th Sephirah, Chesed, to the 3rd Sephirah, Binah). This can be done only with the spiritual guidance of the Angel.

The Abyss is a cosmic looking-glass which reflects the pure, ideal concepts of the First Trinity creating the illusion of a Second Trinity (which in turn extrudes the even more unreal Third Trinity). One could say, with relative accuracy, that the seven Sephiroth below the Abyss are only shadow worlds and the phenomenal universe is no more "real" than the world you can see behind your image when you look into a mirror.

In the midst of the Abyss is a phantom Sephirah called Daath. Daath is technically not a true Sephirah but an environment of absolute dispersion. It is sometimes referred to as the Crown of Knowledge for this is as high as the mind may climb. To transcend Daath and cross the Abyss the mind must be transcended. Naturally the mind will violently resist this and try to trick itself into thinking that it *has* crossed the Abyss and arrived at Binah. But in fact it has fallen into the Abyss, mistaking Daath for Binah. This mistake is common, particularly among those who have not achieved Knowledge and Conversation of their Holy Guardian Angel nor integrated and explored the lower Sephiroth, but instead have rejected them as banal.

The names of the Sephiroth are as follows:

1. KETHER

(The Crown) The Monad. All subsequent Sephiroth are aspects or qualities of Kether. The Sphere of Primum Mobil. Natural position for the *Aces*.

2. CHOKMAH

(Wisdom) The Father. The sphere of the Zodiac. Natural position for Small Card *Twos* and Court Card *Kings*.

3. BINAH

(Understanding) The Mother. The sphere of Saturn. Natural position for Small Card *Threes* and Court Card *Queens*.

4. CHESED OR GEDULAH

(Mercy) Sphere of Jupiter. Natural position for Small Card *Fours*.

5. GEBURAH OR PACHAD

(Strength) Sphere of Mars. Natural position for Small Card *Fives*.

6. TIPHARETH

(Beauty) sphere of the Sun. Natural position for Small Card *Sixes* and Court Card *Princes*. (This is the Sephirah of *The Holy Guardian Angel*. By referring to the Tree of Life Diagram you will see that Tiphareth is a direct reflection of Kether and reflects directly through Yesod, the astral plane, to Malkuth.)

7. NETZACH

(Victory) sphere of Venus. Natural position for Small Card *Sevens*.

8. HOD

(Splendor) sphere of Mercury, Natural position for Small Card *Eights*.

9. YESOD

(Foundation) sphere of Luna, Natural position for Small Card *Nines*.

10. MALKUTH

(Kingdom) sphere of the Elements, the material world, Earth. Natural position for Small Card *Tens* and Court Card *Princesses*.

There is a Tree of Life for each of the Four Worlds of the Qabalah (Four suits of the Tarot) and, as you can see from the Tree of Life diagram, the Ten Sephiroth are joined by 22 paths which of course are the 22 Trumps of the Major Arcana.

There is also another and more simple way to conceptualize all this by using only one Tree of Life.

Yod, the King, resides in the Second Sephirah, Chokmah.

Heh, the Queen, resides in the Third Sephirah, Binah.

Vau, the Prince, resides simultaneously in the next six Sephiroth: Chesed (4), Geburah (5), Tiphareth (6), Netzach (7), Hod (8) and Yesod (9). But his primary nature is focused in Tiphareth.

Heh (Final), the Princess, resides in the Tenth Sephirah, Malkuth.

Keep in mind that the Tree of Life is not only the blueprint of the vast cosmic creation but is also the blueprint of you.

The above is, regrettably, only the most basic "skimming over" of these wonderful concepts. You are encouraged to avail yourself of the many fine books on the Qabalah that are now available everywhere. Most especially we urge you to carefully study Chapter Ten on the Secret Lover.

CHAPTER SEVEN

DETERMINING YOUR SYMBOLS

Secrets of Western Tantra, (The Original Falcon Press) presents a remarkable method of determining your personal Tarot symbols by adding and reducing the numbers of your complete birth date. If you have already calculated your personal Tarot symbols using that, or any other method with which you are comfortable, do not feel that you are required to adopt the method below. The divinatory process does not pivot on this point and it is far better to stick with tried and true symbols with which you already emotionally identify. The method below is based upon traditional Qabalistic correspondences as used by the Hermetic Order of the Golden Dawn. It conforms with the material, charts and tables of Regardie's *Complete Golden Dawn System Of Magic* (The Original Falcon Press).

Let us begin the process by determining your most abstract yet most powerful symbol:

YOUR ARCHETYPAL SYMBOL
OF THE MAJOR ARCANA

For our purposes we will view the 22 images of the Major Arcana (or the Trumps) as being energies or qualities on a truly Cosmic scale. For the purpose of divination these will sometimes represent major universal influences beyond one's direct control. However, for the purpose of the invocation of your Secret Lover these symbols refer to specific psycho-spiritual-sexual energies that are utilized during the ritual described in Chapter Eleven.

The selection process for your major card is very easy and is simply based on your birth sign.

FINDING YOUR ARCHETYPAL SYMBOL
IN THE MAJOR ARCANA
Tarot Symbol & Birth Sign

The Emperor
ARIES the Ram — Fire Sign
(March 21 to April 20)

Hierophant
TAURUS the Bull — Earth Sign
(April 21 to May 20)

The Lovers
GEMINI the Twins — Air Sign
(May 21 to June 20)

The Chariot
CANCER the Crab — Water Sign
(June 21 to July 21)

Strength
LEO the Lion — Fire Sign
(July 22 to August 22)

The Hermit
VIRGO the Virgin — Earth Sign
(August 23 to Sept. 22)

Justice
LIBRA the Scale — Air Sign
(Sept. 23 to Oct. 22)

Death
SCORPIO the Scorpion — Water Sign
(Oct. 23 to Nov. 22)

Temperance
SAGITTARIUS the Archer — Fire Sign
(Nov. 23 to Dec. 21)

The Devil
CAPRICORN the Goat — Earth Sign
(Dec. 22 to Jan. 19)

The Star
AQUARIUS the Water Bearer — Air Sign
(Jan. 20 to Feb. 18)

The Moon
PISCES the Fishes — Water Sign
(Feb 19 to March 20)

The meanings of these cards and all the cards are found later in the book.

Note: These dates are approximations. There are 360 degrees of the Zodiac and about 365 1/4 days in a year. In any given year these dates may vary by as much as three days. If your birthday is on or near the first or last day of the Sign you should check an ephemeris of the year you were born. This applies to determining *all* your representative cards that follow.

Find the card from the Major Arcana that symbolizes you and write it down in your journal. This journal is very important and will be an essential tool to assure a successful operation.

We both are Cancers so our Archetypal symbol is *The Chariot*. By studying the significance and meanings of your Archetypal card you can discover the primal force which is the underlying foundation of your life.

Your Character Card

Next you must determine your Character card from among 12 of the 16 Court Cards.

But first we will explain a bit about the Court Cards and just how and why they represent us.

As we have learned, the Court Cards and the Small Cards are divided into four Suits; *Wands, Cups, Swords* and *Disks*. These are representative of the four *Elements* that the ancients believed were the building blocks of creation; *Fire, Water, Air,* and *Earth*.

Of course, these are not the chemical elements which combine to form the material world, nor are they literally Fire, Water, Air and Earth. They are, most simply put, the totality of all the forces, energies and qualities in the universe divided into four broad categories.

These elemental qualities are the foundation of both galaxies and sub-atomic particles and the limitless diversity of creation is the result of the almost infinite number of ways these four Elements can be mixed, combined and recombined.

It is interesting that modern physics postulates four primal forces, *the Strong Force, the Electro-Magnetic Force, the Weak Force, and the Gravitational Force,* that characteristically bear a remarkable resemblance to these elemental qualities.

The ancients also postulated a Fifth Element (quite literally a "quintessence") which serves the double duty of binding these four Elements together and, at the same time, keeping them far enough apart so they retain aspects of their individuality. They called this Fifth Element *Spirit*.

56

Spirit is intimately related to the Aces and therefore has a most important place in the Tarot and in our search for our Secret Lover.

Each of us when we were born, entered the dimension of this Elemental world. As such the date of our birth is much like our *landing coordinates* and marks our creation on this plane of existence. The first and most general characteristic of this "landmark of our creation" is our Zodiac (Sun) Sign. The Tarot symbol of this Sign (Our Archetypal Symbol of the Major Arcana) we have already determined above.

The next symbol, the Character Card, is more specific and personal: it reveals qualities of personality and individual tendencies. It provides a more specialized definition of our character than our Zodiac symbol.

Like the 12 Zodiacal cards of the Major Arcana, each of the four Kings, four Queens, and four Princes are allocated to 1/12th of the Zodiac or 30° of the year.

[Note: Princesses by tradition are not allocated to degrees of the Zodiac (Time coordinates) but, with the Aces, rule over the four quadrants surrounding the North Pole of the Earth (Space co-ordinates). They actually serve as the Thrones of the Aces.]

Unlike the Zodiac cards of the Major Arcana which represent the three decans (30° of their respective sign), the Court cards rule the three decans from 20° of one Sign to 20° of the next. In this way we can see the beginning of the Divine churning process which characterizes the elemental universe and which will eventually filter down to us to manifest in our own personalities and the personalities of others.

As we saw earlier, the four members of the Court Card "family", the King, the Queen, the Prince and the Princess also represent the four Elements.

The Kings represent the Fire quality of their respective suit while the Queens represent the Water quality, the Princes represent the Air quality and the Princesses represent the Earth quality of their respective suit:

King of Wands
Represents **Fire** of **Fire**
Queen of Wands
Represents **Water** of **Fire**
Prince of Wands
Represents **Air** of **Fire**
Princess of Wands
Represents **Earth** of **Fire**

King of Cups
Represents **Fire** of **Water**
Queen of Cups
Represents **Water** of **Water**
Prince of Cups
Represents **Air** of **Water**
Princess of Cups
Represents **Earth** of **Water**

King of Swords
Represents **Fire** of **Air**
Queen of Swords
Represents **Water** of **Air**
Prince of Swords
Represents **Air** of **Air**
Princess of Swords
Represents **Earth** of **Air**

King of Disks
  Represents **Fire** of **Earth**
Queen of **Disks**
  Represents **Water** of **Earth**
Prince of **Disks**
  Represents **Air** of **Earth**
Princess of Disks
  Represents **Earth** of **Earth**

Your Character card is also calculated by your birth date and is very easy to determine.

FINDING YOUR CHARACTER SYMBOL
IN THE COURT CARDS

March 11—April 10   *Queen of Wands*
  20° Pisces to 20° Aries

April 11—May 10   *Prince of Disks*
  20° Aries to 20° Taurus

May 11—June 10   *King of Swords*
  20° Taurus to 20° Gemini

June 11—July 11   *Queen of Cups*
  20° Gemini to 20° Cancer

July 12—August 11   *Prince of Wands*
  20° Cancer to 20° Leo

August 12—September 11   *King of Disks*
  20° Leo to 20° Virgo

September 12—October 12   *Queen of Swords*
  20° Virgo to 20° Libra

October 13—November 12   *Prince of Cups*
  20° Libra to 20° Scorpio

November 13—December 12   *King of Wands*
     20° Scorpio to 20° Sagittarius

December 13—January 9   *Queen of Disks*
     20° Sagittarius to 20° Capricorn

January 10—February 8   *Prince of Swords*
     20° Capricorn to 20° Aquarius

February 9—March 10   *King of Cups*
     20° Aquarius to 20° Pisces

Find the Court Card that symbolizes you and write it down in your journal.

Mr. DuQuette's birthday is July 11 so his Character Card is the *Queen of Cups*. Dr. Hyatt's birthday is July 12 so his Character Card is the *Prince of Wands*.

Note: It makes absolutely no difference if your Character symbol is not the same gender as you are. These symbols transcend gender, sexual traits and tendencies. For example, both Elizabeth Taylor and George Harrison are the *King of Cups*.

When studying the characteristics of your Character Card later in this book you will most likely recognize many facets of your own character. Then again, you may recognize very little of yourself in the description of your card. Meditate on those qualities you recognize in yourself and those that you do not. If you feel strongly that the your card is so far off in its description of your character that you can't possibly identify with it, use the method described below to find your Character Symbol. No matter how you make your choice, once you've decided, stick with it.

Alternative Method Of Determining
Your Character Symbol

Generalities

Man, over 40,	*King* force
Woman, over 40,	*Queen* force
Man, under 40,	*Prince* force
Woman, under 40,	*Princess* force

If The Birth Sign Is Known

Fire Signs (Aries, Leo, Sagittarius)

Man over 40	*King of Wands*
Woman over 40	*Queen of Wands*
Man under 40	*Prince of Wands*
Woman under 40	*Princess of Wands*

Water Signs (Cancer, Scorpio, Pisces)

Man over 40	*King of Cups*
Woman over 40	*Queen of Cups*
Man under 40	*Prince of Cups*
Woman under 40	*Princess of Cups*

Air Signs (Gemini, Libra, Aquarius)

Man over 40	*King of Swords*
Woman over 40	*Queen of Swords*
Man under 40	*Prince of Swords*
Woman under 40	*Princess of Swords*

Earth Signs (Taurus, Virgo, Capricorn)

Man over 40	*King of Disks*
Woman over 40	*Queen of Disks*
Man under 40	*Prince of Disks*
Woman under 40	*Princess of Disks*

Now we turn to the remaining forty cards of the Minor Arcana. These are Ace through 10 of each of the four suites.

The Four Aces: The Root Symbol

As we have mentioned earlier, the Aces are unique and represent not the elements themselves, but the "root" or "seed" of the elements.

The Aces will play an important part in the Ultimate Divination. But for the time being simply find the root card that represents you.

Determining Your Root Symbol

Your Root Symbol is the Ace of the Element that rules your Archetypal Symbol (Zodiac Sign) as found in the chart above. To review briefly;

Wands are Fire signs: *Aries, Leo, Sagittarius*
Cups are Water signs: *Cancer, Scorpio, Pisces*
Swords are Air signs: *Gemini, Aquarius, Libra*
Disks are Earth signs: *Taurus, Capricorn, Virgo*

We are both Cancers which is a Water sign so our Root Symbol is the Ace of Cups. (Scorpio and Pisces people would also be the Ace of Cups) This also means we have a special affinity with all the Water cards.

Find the Root Symbol Card that symbolizes you and write it down in your journal.

Now we will turn our attention to the remaining 36 small cards of the Minor Arcana.

Your Personal Symbol

The belt of the Zodiac and its corresponding houses is divided naturally into 360°. As we have seen above, each of the 12 signs contains 30° which is divided further into 3 parts, (or Decans) of 10°.

Each of the 36 small cards represents one of these 36 Decans or approximately ten days of the year. Your Personal Symbol card is simply determined by locating the Decan of your birth-date.

Instead of representing Cosmic influences—like your Archetypal-Trump card—or personality traits—like your Character-Court card—the Personal symbol card represents, to a certain extent, the challenges of your incarnation—your karmic baggage.

Each of the decans, by tradition, has specific characteristics based upon its relative position in the Zodiac. Familiarity with the card of your natal decan can help you understand the specific qualities and nature of your spiritual energy.

Dr. Hyatt's birthday (July 12) makes him a *4 of Cups* which is the *Luxury* card. At first glance this seems like a very attractive card to be, and indeed it is. But like all the small cards it presents him with three things; a *blessing*, a *curse* and the *means* to overcome them both.

For example: living in the "lap of luxury" could be the fulfillment of a dream and the reward for work well done or it can represent a seductive trap that would allow you to do absolutely nothing worthwhile with your life. J. Paul Getty manifested the "blessing" of luxury by creating one of the most beautiful art museums in the world. But Siddhartha, by overcoming the "curse" of luxury, became the Buddha.

Mr. DuQuette's card the *3 of Cups: Abundance* exhibits similar characteristics but with more emphasis on emotional rather than material qualities.

This dual nature of the decans is underscored by the fact that Qabalists assign a pair of angels to each decan, one to rule the day the other the night. The 72 spirits of the Goetia are also delegated in pairs to each of the 36 decans.

Don't be too quick to dismiss the relevancy or accuracy of your Personal Symbol Card or feel that you have been cheated if you happen to be a grim symbol like the *Defeat* or *Sorrow* card. As a matter of fact if it makes you somewhat uncomfortable it may be touching an important "nerve". No Tarot card, in itself, is "lucky" or "unlucky" and the Ultimate Divination as outlined in this book is not an exercise in "fortune telling" but instead an essential part of knowing your Secret Lover.

Finding Your Personal Symbol
in the Minor Arcana

ARIES

March 21—March 30
  2 of Wands   *Dominion*
March 31—April 10
  3 of Wands   *Virtue*
April 11—April 20
  4 of Wands   *Completion*

TAURUS

April 21—April 30
  5 of Disks   *Worry*
May 1—May 10
  6 of Disks   *Success*
May 11—May 20
  7 of Disks   *Failure*

GEMINI

May 21—May 31
    8 of Swords   *Interference*
June 1—June 10
    9 of Swords   *Cruelty*
June 11—June 20
    10 of Swords   *Ruin*

CANCER

June 21—July 1
    2 of Cups   *Love*
July 2—July 11
    3 of Cups   *Abundance*
July 12—July 21
    4 of Cups   *Luxury*

LEO

July 22—August 1
    5 of Wands   *Strife*
August 2—August 11
    6 of Wands   *Victory*
August 12—August 22
    7 of Wands   *Valor*

VIRGO

August 23—September 1
    8 of Disks   *Prudence*
September 2—September 11
    9 of Disks   *Gain*
September 12—September 22
    10 of Disks   *Wealth*

LIBRA

September 23—October 2
   2 of Swords   *Peace*
October 3—October 12
   3 of Swords   *Sorrow*
October 13—October 22
   4 of Swords   *Truce*

SCORPIO

October 23—November 1
   5 of Cups   *Disappointment*
November 2—November 12
   6 of Cups   *Pleasure*
November 13—November 22
   7 of Cups   *Debauch*

SAGITTARIUS

November 23—December 2
   8 of Wands   *Swiftness*
December 3—12
   9 of Wands   *Strength*
December 13—December 21
   10 of Wands   *Oppression*

CAPRICORN

December 22—December 30
   2 of Disks   *Change*
December 31—January 9
   3 of Disks   *Works*
January 10—January 19
   4 of Disks   *Power*

AQUARIUS

January 20—January 29
   5 of Swords   *Defeat*
January 30—February 8
   6 of Swords   *Science*
February 9—February 18
   7 of Swords   *Futility*

PISCES

February 19—February 28
   8 of Cups   *Indolence*
March 1—March 10
   9 of Cups   *Happiness*
March 11—March 20
   10 of Cups   *Satiety*

If your birth-date is April 15, your Personal Symbol is the *4 of Wands*. If it is February 10, it is the *7 of Swords*, etc.

Find the Personal Symbol Card that symbolizes you and write it down in your journal.

THE PRECEDING PERSONAL SYMBOL & THE PROGRESSIVE PERSONAL SYMBOL

Your Preceding Personal card is the small card that appears sequentially just before your Personal Card and your Progressive Personal Symbol is the Card that comes immediately after your Personal Card.

You will notice that in the chart above the Tarot symbols progress through the decans in a peculiar manner. While the numbers 2 through 10 continue in sequence, they also are passing, in groups of threes, through the four Elemental Suits. This is a continuation of the elemental *churning* process that we saw beginning with the Court Cards.

67

In determining your Proceeding Personal Symbol and your Progressive Personal Symbol we *do not use the chart above* but simply use the number sequence of the small cards themselves.

2–10 of Wands,
2–10 of Cups,
2–10 of Swords,
2–10 of Disks.

The Preceding minor arcana symbol gives you a sense of where you are coming from. Your Personal card indicates where you are. And the Progressive symbol tells you what follows. These are not simply the *past*, *present* and the *future*, but rather they should be viewed as three pages of a "flip cartoon" or three consecutive frames of motion picture film. The *movement* that is exhibited by these three cards can tell you a great deal about yourself, your tendencies and perhaps give you a clue to your True Will.

As Dr. Hyatt is the *4 of Cups*, his Preceding Personal Symbol is the *3 of Cups* and his Progressive Personal Symbol is the *5 of Cups*. As the four, he is in the middle moving about these three symbols. This can tell him much about how he functions and the events of his daily life.

Note: Determining your Preceding and Progressive Personal Symbols, if you are a 10 or a 2, is a little different. If, for example, you are a 10 of Wands, your Preceding card is the 9 of Wands but your Progressive card is the 2 of *Cups*. This is based on the rule of descending worlds. Thus moving down from the suite of Fire (Wands) you move into the suite of Water (Cups). In the *10 of Wands*, the balancing symbols for the past and future would be the *9 of Wands* and *2 of Cups* respectively.

If you are the *10 of Disks,* your Preceding symbol would be, of course, the *9 of Disks,* but your Progressive symbol would be the *2 of Wands.* In other words, when your reach the "bottom" your start again at the top.

Now write down your Preceding and Progressive Personal Symbols in your journal.

In my opinion, this is the finest way of studying the psycho-spiritual notion of karma. In fact, students who employ these symbols as Karmic keys begin to develop a large amount of free will. For some this will enable them to move through all their lives in one lifetime and free themselves from the wheel of birth and re-birth.

In understanding the evolution of a soul we can theorize that we all start from the world of Fire (Wands) and move to the world of Earth (Disks). Disk people could be viewed as being closer to finishing their tour of duty than any of the other suits.

Or one might speculate that the Fire people (Wands) are closer to finishing their tour than any other. Since this is a model that no one can verify, the safest method is to learn to live the life of each symbol in the minor cards.

Now, in Dr. Hyatt's journal for example he would have the following symbols:

Birth date: July 12, 1943
Archetypal Symbol: The Chariot
Character Symbol: Prince of Wands
Root Symbol: Ace of Cups
Personal Symbol: Four of Cups
Preceding Personal Symbol: Three of Cups
Progressive Personal Symbol: Five of Cups

If, for a moment, you can imagine a force starting somewhere in the Universe and finding its way down to a single point, you will get a sense of the Archetypal energy moving its way from the Major Symbol, to the Court Symbol to the Root Symbol of the Ace and then down to your Personal Symbols.

Using the above symbols you can now begin to create a story about your self and your present situation. Below is an example of such a story that Dr. Hyatt wrote in his journal. You should do the same thing for yourself.

> As the *Charioteer* I am archetypically involved with the abstract aspects of Triumph and Victory over certain powerful forces. Being at the "reigns" of the elemental forces that propel the chariot of my life is very important to me. As *Prince of Wands* I find myself still driving a chariot, this time pulled by the Lion of my Will. This manifests in my character (which I like to think of as noble and generous), but when my "lion" is not tightly reined, I am impulsive, and sometimes violently opinionated and capable of great extremes of emotion. The Fire/Air nature of the *Prince of Wands* is displayed in my character by my enthusiasm for writing. But my real passion, the science of Tantric Love and the quest for my Secret Lover, is reflected perfectly by my Root Card, the *Ace of Cups* and its association with Holy Grail, the Moon and the Sacred Yoni.
>
> My Personal Card, the *4 of Cups* (Luxury), indicates a certain level of stability and comfort in my environment. However, if I look at the sequence of my Preceding Card, the *3 of Cups* (Abundance), and my Progressive Card, *The 5 of Cups* (Disappointment), I see a cliché "morality" drama unfolding: Abundance, Luxury, Disappointment. This indeed is a continual source of "food for thought" and a

70

constant reminder to use the abundance of the "good things" of my life to further my Great Work and not be dazzled into dissipating activities or—worse—inactivity.

Of course, the foregoing is only a very brief description. Meditation on these symbols is a life-long process. I have found that by using my personal Tarot symbols as a part of my daily meditations I have become more conscious of their effect on my day-to-day activities.

Look at the symbols that precede and follow *your* birth symbol in the Minor Arcana. (Your Personal Symbol) and you will begin to create your own "karmic-genetic file cabinet" and see your own story unfold.

Later on, focus on the symbols that precede and follow you in the Major Arcana. These can be found in their sequential order elsewhere in this book. Though these are highly abstract and archetypal, they will give you clues to the nature of your Psyche.

CHAPTER EIGHT

THE MEANINGS OF THE CARDS

Each Tarot card is the visual representation of 1/78th of the Infinite Reality. It follows then, (the nature of Infinity being what it is), that each card has infinite aspects and, (if we were burdened with omniscience), infinite meaning.

But, thank the gods, we are not as yet cursed with such a mental capacity. But unfortunately we *are* endowed with just enough gray matter to find ourselves in an almost perpetual state of confusion whenever we start to define and analyze infinite concepts. This is why the visual images of the Tarot are so valuable to us. They work upon the right side the brain where concepts transcending intellectual analysis can be processed. In passing it might also be said that the Holy Guardian Angel or the Secret Lover is a right brain phenomenon.

Western Tantric interpretations of the Major Arcana are provided for specific applications mentioned in Chapter Eleven. The general meanings of the Tarot cards that we present below are very brief and provide only the most basic key words of definition. Some of these are taken, from information provided to initiates of the Golden Dawn while others are suggested from the writings of Aleister Crowley. The reader is advised to make a continual study of the Tarot and take every opportunity to review the many fine works of other

73

authors. Especially recommend are the works of Aleister Crowley and Paul Foster Case.

BRIEF MEANINGS OF THE TAROT TRUMPS

Note: In the following pages, the number that appears before the name of each card is called the *Key Number* and dictates the sequence of cards. This should not be confused with the numerical value of the Hebrew letter designated for each card.

You will find three types of "meanings" attributed to each of the Tarot Trumps. The first is poetic (for the right side of the brain) and is from Crowley's masterpiece of Tarot, *The Book of Thoth*; the second is "Tantric" for the Ritual of the Secret Lover; and the third is the classic divinitory meaning.

Christopher S. Hyatt, Ph.D. • Lon Milo DuQuette

0. THE FOOL

Hebrew letter: א Aleph, (Ox)

Numerical Value: 1. Element: **AIR**
Path from Kether to Chokmah
Full Title: The Spirit of the Æthyr
KNOW NAUGHT! ALL WAYS ARE LAWFUL TO INNOCENCE. PURE FOLLY IS THE KEY TO INITIATION. SILENCE BREAKS INTO RAPTURE.
The purest impulse toward Union between the Macrocosm and Microcosm.
Idea, thought, spirituality, that which endeavors to rise above the material.

75

1. THE MAGICIAN

Hebrew letter: ‎ב‎ Beth, (House)
Numerical Value: 2, Planet: **MERCURY**
Path from Kether to Binah
Full Title: The Magus of Power
The True Self is the meaning of the True Will: know Thyself through Thy Way. Calculate well the Formula of Thy Way. Create freely; absorb joyously; divide intently; consolidate completely. Work thou, Omnipotent, Omniscient, Omnipresent, in and for Eternity.
The archetypal Mage: the Male Counter Part of the Universal Will toward Union. He is continuous never-ending creation. The Supreme male image of the Secret Lover.
Skill, wisdom, mastery of the Elements, adaptation craft, cunning, etc. Sometimes occult wisdom.

2. THE HIGH PRIESTESS

Hebrew letter: ג Gimel, (Camel)

Numerical Value: 3, Planet: **MOON**

Path from Kether to Tiphareth.

Full Title: The Priestess of the Silver Star

Purity is to live only to the Highest; and the Highest is All; be thou as Artemis to Pan. Read thou in the Book of the Law, and break through the veil of the Virgin.

The archetypal Vessel: the Female Counter Part of the Universal Will toward Union. The Supreme female image of the Secret Lover.

The Divine Vessel, change, alteration, increase and decrease, fluctuation. Compare with Death and Moon Cards.

3. THE EMPRESS

Hebrew letter: ד Daleth, (Door)
Numerical Value: 4, Planet: **VENUS**
Path from Chokmah to Binah.
Full Title: The Daughter of the Mighty Ones
This is the Harmony of the Universe, that Love unites the Will to create with the Understanding of that Creation: understand thou thine own Will. Love and let love. Rejoice in every shape of love, and get thy rapture and thy nourishment thereof.
The symbol of the Veil as it blossoms forth with the Creative Waters of Heaven. The Universal Womb with Child—The Symbol of Coming and Going—Vagina—The Door of Life.
Beauty, happiness, pleasure, success, also luxury and sometimes dissipation.

4. THE EMPEROR

Hebrew letter: ה Heh, (Window)

Numerical Value: 5, Zodiac Sign: **ARIES**

Path from Chokmah to Tiphareth

Full Title: Sun of the Morning, Chief among the Mighty

Use all thine energy to rule thy thought: burn up thy thought as the Phoenix.

The Secret Lover as Spiritual Conqueror. The driving force of Love. The male image of the Holy Guardian Angel as Initiator of Union.

War, conquest, victory, strife, ambition. Note: See THE STAR for Thelemic attribution.

5. THE HIEROPHANT

Hebrew letter: ו Vau, (Nail)

Numerical Value: 6, Zodiac Sign: **TAURUS**

Path from Chokmah to Chesed.

Full Title: The Magus of the Eternal

Offer thyself Virgin to the Knowledge and Conversation of thine Holy Guardian Angel. All else is a snare. Be thou athlete with the eight limbs of Yoga: for without these thou are not disciplined for any fight.

The classic image of the Secret Lover as spirit in action, often manifesting as the Voice of the Secret Lover.

The inner voice, divine wisdom, manifestation, explanation, teaching, occult wisdom, differing from though resembling in some respects, The Magician, The Hermit, and The Lovers.

6. THE LOVERS

Hebrew letter: ‫ז‬ Zayin, (Sword)

Numerical Value: 7, Zodiac Sign: **GEMINI**

Path from Binah to Tiphareth.

Full Title: The Children of the Voice: the Oracle of the Mighty Gods

The Oracle of the Gods is the Child-Voice of Love in Thine own Soul; hear thou it. Heed not the Siren-Voice of Sense, or the Phantom-Voice of Reason: rest in Simplicity, and listen to the Silence.

High Priestess (2) and Hierophant (5) as Tantric Lovers (7)

Inspiration Motive, power, and action, arising from inspiration and impulse.

7. THE CHARIOT

Hebrew letter: ‎ח Cheth, (Fence)

Numerical Value: 8, Zodiac Sign: **CANCER**

Path from Binah to Geburah

Full Title: The Child of the Powers of the Waters: the Lord of the Triumph of Light

The Issue of the Vulture, Two-in-One, conveyed; this is the Chariot of Power. TRINC: the last oracle.

The Knight and Bearer of the Holy Graal.

The Great Work accomplished, triumph, victory, health. Success though sometimes not stable and enduring.

82

8. STRENGTH (LUST)

Hebrew letter: ט Teth, (Serpent)

Numerical Value: 9, Zodiac Sign: **LEO**
Path from Chesed to Geburah.
Full Title: The Daughter of the Flaming Sword
Mitigate Energy with Love; but let Love devour all things. Worship the name—-, foursquare, mystic, wonderful, and the name of His House 418.
The Kundalini aroused and controlled.
Courage, strength, fortitude. Power not arrested as in the act of Judgment, but passing on to further action, sometimes obstinacy, etc. Compare with 11 Justice. *(In former times and in other decks 8 Justice and 11 Strength were transposed.)*

9. THE HERMIT

Hebrew letter: ' Yod, (Hand)

Numerical Value: 10, Zodiac Sign: **VIRGO**

Path from Chesed to Tiphareth.

Full Title: The Prophet of the Eternal, the Magus of the Voice of Power

Wander alone; bearing the Light and thy Staff. And be the Light so bright that no man seeth thee. Be not moved by aught without or within: keep Silence in all ways.

Sperm and the secret location in the body where it is produced.

Wisdom sought for and obtained from above. Divine Inspiration (but active as opposed to that of the Lovers). Can represent the solitary sexual experience.

10. THE WHEEL OF FORTUNE

Hebrew letter: כ Kaph, (Palm of Hand)

Numerical Value: 20, Planet: **Jupiter**

Path from Chesed to Netzach.

Full Title: The Lord of the Forces of Life

Follow thy Fortune, careless where it lead thee. The axle moveth not: attain thou that.

The peace which is the precursor to Surrender.

Good fortune and happiness (within bounds), but sometimes also a species of intoxication with success.

11. JUSTICE

Hebrew letter: ל Lamed, (Ox Goad)
Numerical Value: 30, Zodiac: Sign **Libra**
Path from Geburah to Tiphareth.
Full Title: The Daughter of the Lords of Truth. The Ruler of the
Balance
**Balance against each thought its exact opposite. For the Marriage of these
is the Annihilation of Illusion.**
The extended Phallus directed by Will.
Eternal justice and balance. Strength and Force, but arrested as in
the act of Judgment. Compare with 8 Strength.

12. THE HANGED MAN

Hebrew letter: ‫מ‬ Mem, (Water)
Numerical Value: 40, Element: **WATER**
Path from Geburah to Hod.
Full Title: The Spirit of the Mighty Waters
Let not the waters whereon thou journeyest wet thee. And, being come to shore, plant thou the Vine and rejoice without shame.
The Medium of Ego-Loss.
Life suspended upon the Water, voluntary but most often enforced sacrifice.

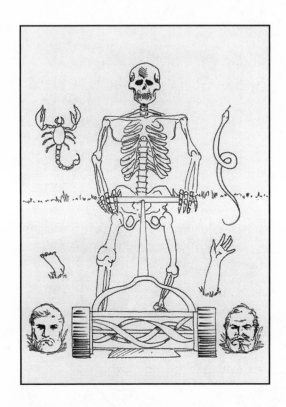

13. DEATH

Hebrew letter: ‫ב‬ Nun, (Fish)
Numerical Value: 50, Zodiac Sign: **SCORPIO**
Path from Tiphareth to Netzach.
Full Title: The Child of the Great Transformers.
The Universe is Change; every Change is the effect of an Act of Love; all Acts of Love contain Pure Joy. Die daily. Death is the apex of one curve of the snake Life: behold all opposites as necessary complements, and rejoice.
Putrefaction of the Ego and non-essentials in preparation for the Secret Lover.
The womb of time, ages, transformation, involuntary change. Sometimes death and destruction. Compare also with High Priestess.

14. TEMPERANCE (ART)

Hebrew letter: ס Samech (Prop)

Numerical Value : 60, Zodiac Sign: **SAGITTARIUS**

Path from Tiphareth to Yesod.

Full Title: The Daughter of the Reconcilers, the Bringer-forth of Life

Pour thine all freely from the Vase in thy right hand and lose no drop. Hath not thy left hand a vase? Transmute all wholly into the Image of thy Will, bringing each to its true token of Perfection. Dissolve the Pearl in the Wine-cup: and make manifest the Virtue of that Pearl.

The Union of Opposites—The Alchemical Marriage—the transub-stantiation of the Elements of the Elixir of Life.

Combination of Forces. Realization. Action (material). The alchemical accomplishment of the Great Work.

15. THE DEVIL

Hebrew letter: ע Ayin, (Eye)

Numerical Value: 70, Zodiac Sign: **CAPRICORN**

Path from Tiphareth to Yesod.

Full Title: The Lord of the Gates of Matter. The Child of the Forces of Time

With thy right Eye create all for thyself, and with the left accept all that be created otherwise.

The meatus—the eye of the phallus. The Window to the World of Darkness.

Lust materialism, material force, material temptation; sometimes obsession.

16. THE TOWER STRUCK

Hebrew letter: פ Pe, (Mouth)
Numerical Value: 80, Planet: **MARS**
Path from Netzach to Hod.
Full Title: The Lord of the Hosts of the Mighty
Break down the fortress of thine Individual Self, that thy Truth may spring free from the ruins.
The annihilation of the Ego in orgasm with the Secret Lover. The means by which the Sacrament is gathered.
Ambition, fighting, war, courage. Compare with Emperor. In certain combinations, destruction, danger, fall, ruin.

17. THE STAR

Hebrew letter: צ Tzaddi, (Fish-Hook)
Numerical Value: 90, Zodiac Sign: **AQUARIUS**
Path from Netzach to Yesod.
Full Title: The Daughter of the Firmament: the Dweller between the Waters.
Pure water on thyself: thus shalt thou be a Fountain to the Universe. Find thou thyself in every Star. Achieve thou every possibility.
Meditation has been transcended. The Trance is viewing you.
The Star Goddess, Nuit, "the naked brilliance of the voluptuous night-sky." Note: Thelemic tradition assigns Hebrew letter Heh to THE STAR and Tzaddi to the Emperor.

18. THE MOON

Hebrew letter: ק Qoph, (Back of Head)
Numerical Value: 100, Zodiac Sign: **PISCES**
Path from Netzach to Malkuth.
Full Title: The ruler of the Flux and Reflux. The Child of the Sons of the Mighty
Let the Illusion of the World pass over thee, unheeded, as thou goest from the Midnight to the Morning.
The menstrual fluids. The cycle of disappointment which leads again to ever lasting life.
The ebb and flow of life, dissatisfaction, voluntary change (as opposed to Death). Error, lying, falsity, deception.

19. THE SUN

Hebrew letter: ‏ר‎ Resh, (Head)

Numerical Value: 200, Planet: **SUN**

Path from Hod to Yesod.

Full Title: The Lord of the Fire of the World

Give forth thy light to all without doubt; the clouds and shadows are no matter for thee. Make Speech and Silence, Energy and Stillness, twin forms of thy play.

The radiant image of the Holy Guardian Angel.

Glory, Gain, Riches. Sometimes also arrogance. Display. Sometimes vanity.

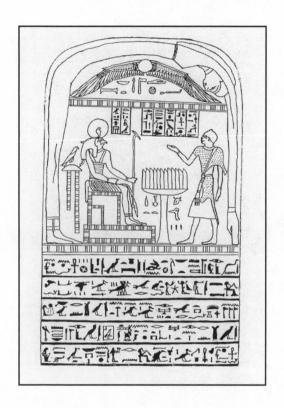

20. JUDGMENT (AEON)

Hebrew letter: ש Shin, (Tooth)

Numerical Value: 300, Element(s): **FIRE/SPIRIT**

Path from Hod to Malkuth.

Full Title: The Spirit of the Primal Fire

Be every Act an Act of Love and Worship. Be every Act the Fiat of a God. Be every Act a Source of radiant Glory.

The Holy Ghost that descends upon the Graal.

Final decision. Judgment. Sentence. Determination of a matter without appeal on its plane.

95

21. THE WORLD

Hebrew letter: ת Tav, (Tau Cross)

Numerical Value: 400, Planet: **SATURN**, Element: **EARTH**

Path from Yesod to Malkuth

Full Title: The Great One of the Night of Time

Treat time and all conditions of Event as Servants of thy Will, appointed to present the Universe to thee in the form of thy Plan. And: blessing and worship to the prophet of the lovely Star.

The final reabsorption of life. Combined with the Fool—the essence of the Secret Lover ritual.

The matter itself. Synthesis. World. Kingdom. Usually denotes the actual subject of the question.

MEANINGS OF THE MINOR ARCANA & COURT CARDS

Because my training has been in the psycho-social-spiritual aspects of the human condition, I tend to view each of the Minor Arcana symbols as representative of the types of experiences and orientations a person can have in life.

The standard meanings I have given cannot begin to reflect the impact these images have on the mind. In my opinion these images are the best representation of the character, learning experiences and the ups and downs of life. The minor cards, when properly understood, can also offer solutions for the everyday problems of life.

WANDS

The Intuitive Person

King of Wands: Active, generous, fierce, sudden and impetuous; tendency for quick, impulsive and unpredictable actions but if success is not immediate, there is no energy left for follow-through; if ill-dignified this King becomes evil-minded, cruel, brutal. (Note: "Ill-dignified" means that the cards next to it exert a negative influence.)

Queen of Wands: Activity characterized by authoritative, calm persistence; attractive power; kind and generous when not opposed; friendly and loving if on her own terms; can be a snob if ill-dignified, the force is domineering, revengeful, and tyrannical. In a pouting fit she will "cut off her nose to spite her face." This Queen can be a betrayer!

Prince of Wands: Strong, indefatigable character, intensely noble and generous; he is at once an historical romantic and a philosophic visionary; can amuse himself by being a mysterious even terrifying figure or a boisterous braggart. If ill-dignified, he is cruel, intolerant, prejudiced and ill-natured.

Princess of Wands: Brilliance, courage, beauty, force sudden in anger or love; a desire for power; enthusiastic, and revengeful. If ill-dignified, she is superficial, theatrical, cruel, unstable and domineering.

Ace of Wands: Root of fire, force, strength, sudden acceleration. The realm of spirit, creation and energy.

2 of Wands: DOMINION, power over one's sphere and territory.

3 of Wands: VIRTUE, established strength, fixed and entrenched, an aspect of arrogance.

4 of Wands: COMPLETION, perfected and exemplary work, that which endures, equilibrium, balance and harmony.

5 of Wands: STRIFE, clashes and discord with a farcical or absurd quality; impotent, feeble and inept conflict. Compare with the 5 of Swords.

6 of Wands: VICTORY, after stasis; triumph and fulfillment, gain and success.

7 of Wands: VALOR, and fortitude in the face of opposition; however, this may be a false battle, or one created by one's own unconscious temperament.

[By the date reduction method this card is the designated symbol of December 7, 1941, Pearl Harbor Day. This symbol seems most appropriate from the U.S. point of view. (See 9 of Wands)]

8 of Wands: SWIFTNESS, arrival of information with haste, capricious and flighty quality; falling to earth.

9 of Wands: STRENGTH, magnificent strength, outstanding force, health, energy.

[By the Qabalistic method of date reckoning this is the designated symbol of December 7th, Pearl Harbor Day. (This symbol seems most appropriate from the Japanese point of view.)]

10 of Wands: OPPRESSION, revenge, malice, burdens. Here one must learn to calm the mind when oppressed, and take one thing at a time. Magnificent strength has now turned into a burden. What was missing for this to happen?

CUPS
The Feeling Person

King of Cups: Passive, graceful and likable character; naturally pure and innocent; can quickly respond to arousal but sometimes needs help to stick with a project or a relationship; but once inspired carries on with a quiet passion.

If ill-dignified, he is indolent, sensual, idle and untruthful.

Queen of Cups: Pure, beautiful and dreamy character so reflective that she mirrors the qualities of others so well her own imaginative and poetic characteristics often stay concealed. She is popular because she brings out the narcissism in others. If ill-dignified these images are distorted and she mirrors the worst in others.

Prince of Cups: A calm and seemingly mellow facade conceals the true character of an intensely passionate and crafty manipulator. Strong willed, subtle and violent always with an artistic flare. If ill-dignified he is devoid of conscience. and can become intensely evil. (Machiavellian) The Borgia Pope.

Princess of Cups: Sweet, kind, poetic, gentle, imaginative, dreamy, at times indolent, yet courageous if roused. Ill-dignified, she is selfish and luxurious.

Ace of Cups: Root of water, fertility, productiveness, beauty, pleasure and happiness. Creative energy of the heart and emotions.

2 of Cups: LOVE, friendship, marriage; positive emotion, with a quality of courage.

3 of Cups: ABUNDANCE, merriment, joyous friendship; a very feminine energy.

4 of Cups: LUXURY, pleasure, gifts given and received; but some tension always present. Indicates a change in life orientation. Indecision; doubt; Hamlet's hesitation.

5 of Cups: DISAPPOINTMENT, loss of pleasure, disappointment in relationships, nostalgia for the lost things of the past. A person crying behind a closed door.

6 of Cups: PLEASURE, childhood dreams fulfilled. A tendency to live in the past. Sexual Will fulfilled. The joys and games of childhood. The drifter or Flower child.

7 of Cups: DEBAUCH, illusory success, weakness in a position of power, lies, deceit, flattery. There is a strong aspect of self-deception. Believing that the ego is capable of handling responsibility when it is not.

8 of Cups: INDOLENCE, abandoned success, disinterested beginnings, sometimes moving toward the spiritual path. Often referred to as leaving material success for something higher, but not necessarily of ones own free will.

9 of Cups: HAPPINESS, material success complete, wishes fulfilled, sometimes with over-indulgence. Pleasant and generous, but sometimes very moody and greedy (insecure).

10 of Cups: SATIETY, perpetual success, good fortune, This can become very boring if a new challenge and a higher goal is not on the horizon.

SWORDS
The Reasoning Person

King of Swords: Active, subtle, clever, delicate, courageous; inclined to dominate; a storm of energy channeled to practical ends; if ill-dignified he can be indecisive, impotently violent, deceitful, tyrannical and crafty.

Queen of Swords: Highly perceptive, keen mind, very accurate in superficial analysis, quick, subtle; the most graceful of the Court Cards; has excellent balance, can be a skilled dancer. If ill-dignified, she is cruel, sly and deceitful, unreliable, although she puts on a good show.

Prince of Swords: An idea man; the ideal debater; propounder of a myriad of unrelated and often impractical ideas; an intensely clever mind "all dressed up" but often with "no place to go"; he can be distrustful, suspicious, firm in a friendship, careful, slow and over cautious. He can slay as fast as he creates. If ill-dignified, he is harsh, malicious, plotting, obstinate, and unreliable.

Princess of Swords: strength and subtleness in material things. Grace in motion. She can be very frivolous and cunning when needy.

Ace of Swords: Root of air, an invoked force, a great power for good or evil, strength through trouble, the affirmation of justice. The creative energy of reason.

2 of Swords: PEACE, peace restored with minor tension.

3 of Swords: SORROW, deep tears, emotional pain.

4 of Swords: TRUCE, rest after strife, change for the better, a need for quiet time.

5 of Swords: DEFEAT, conflict: victory or defeat, slander, an active card, unlike the 5 of Wands.

6 of Swords: SCIENCE, earned success, a journey ended, hard work leads to help and success. Indicates a need for movement or association with water, to balance the limitations of reason.

7 of Swords: FUTILITY, unstable effort, untrustworthiness: impulsive, greedy action. A symbol of deviousness if ill-dignified.

8 of Swords: INTERFERENCE, restricted force, petty difficulties; mental manacles; being imprisoned by one's own reasoning process.

9 of Swords: CRUELTY, despair and cruelty, illness of heart: mind at the end of its tether: injustice unexplained. "Why do the nations rage so furiously together, and the people imagine a vain thing?" This card is worse than the following one.

10 of Swords: RUIN, failure, the end of a matter, with the implied hope of a beginning. The worst is over with. Reason has discovered its own end, its own limitations. Man is free from worshipping his logical faculty.

DISKS
The Sensory-Sensual Person

King of Disks: Unless well dignified, he is lazy, heavy, dull and excessive, however he is laborious, clever and patient in material matters. The "salt of the Earth" Successful most often when acting upon instinct. When ill-dignified, he is an avaricious, grasping, dull, jealous and cowardly force.

Queen of Disks: Sensibly ambitious, quietly hard-working kindhearted, domesticated and timid, intelligent but moody; if ill-dignified her life is drudgery; she can be undecided, capricious, foolish, and changeable; prone to drug and alcohol abuse.

Prince of Disks: Solid, reliable and practical in applying his force; ideal "middle management" material because he increases the value of other forces under his control; if ill-dignified he can be unemotional and insensitive even stupid, animal-like and material. He is slow to anger, but when aroused is furious.

Princess of Disks: Generous, kind, diligent, benevolent, careful, courageous, preserving, but sometimes pitiful. If ill-dignified, she is wasteful.

Ace of Disks: Root of earth, material in all senses, both good and evil. It shows material gain, labor, power and wealth. The creative energy of body and earth.

2 of Disks: CHANGE, harmony in the midst of change, pleasant visits, holidays.

3 of Disks: WORK, material work well done, commerce; sometimes a meeting with a teacher.

4 of Disks: POWER, powers over the earth, receiving money but normally with an earthly purpose.

5 of Disks: WORRY, material trouble, loss of property or valuables for those outside of the great work that are assumed to reside within.

6 of Disks: SUCCESS, material success in business.

7 of Disks: FAILURE, successful but unfulfilled, work without reward is successful; unselfish efforts lead to surprise results.

8 of Disks: PRUDENCE, moderation, good skills in handling small matters.

9 of Disks: GAIN, material gain, inheritance.

10 of Disks: WEALTH, on the mundane level; however eventual boredom is very likely.

CHAPTER NINE

ULTIMATE DIVINATION

I invoke thee, IAO, that thou wilt send HRU, the great
Angel that is set over the operations of this Secret Wisdom,
to lay his hand invisibly upon these consecrated cards of art,
that thereby we may obtain true knowledge of hidden
things, to the glory of thine ineffable Name.
Amen.

Divinations of this type are in one sense "not divinations" at all. They are rituals designed to stimulate the
collective mind of the individual and to activate the
powers of Indra's Net. Thus, they should only be used
if the aspirant is sure that he is able to tolerate the type
of forces revealed and is seriously interested in invoking his/her Secret Lover.

The *Ultimate Divination* requires preparation and
should only be employed as a preliminary to the invocation of the Holy Guardian Angel. In this sense the
Ultimate Divination might only be performed once in a
person's life.

As the primary purpose of this divination is the
invocation of your Genius, questions having to do with
understanding your Higher Will or Purpose are the
only questions relevant for this operation.

THE CORRECT TIME

The ideal time to perform this divination is on your
birthday or, if you know it, the date of your concep-

tion. If this is not practical, choose a date that has some significance to you.

Equinoxes, Solstices, and holidays are often significant days. How many times have you heard people say things like; "I remember Christmas of 1982." Or "It was New Years Eve 1974 when I quit smoking and turned my life around." If you are familiar with your horoscope you may choose a time when planetary aspects are favorable or similar to that of your nativity.

THE DAY CARD

The day you pick to perform the Divination Ritual is also represented by a Tarot card called the Day Card. The most obvious choice would be the Small Card that represents the exact decan of the day in question. It is determined in the same way as your Personal Card. Or you may wish to calculate the day card by adding and reducing the numbers. [July 13, 1991 (7 + 13 + 1991 = 130 = 4) Cancer is a Water Sign so July 13, 1991 would be the *4 of Cups*.] it is interesting to note that by both methods of calculation this date works out to be the *4 of Cups*. Obviously it will not always be the case but it does show a harmony between the systems.

You should begin to select your date and time at least one month before you prepare to do the Divination.

We must warn the reader that the impulsive or mundane use of this method will lead to poor results and worse it will create a "bad" mental set toward future workings with your Angel.

PREPARATION

For at least two weeks prior to the Divination perform the ritual of the Middle Pillar and the Meditation of the Seer daily. (See Appendices.)

To communicate more clearly with the Secret Lover it is important that you have a good understanding of yourself. Self honesty is essential to receive the Love and Guidance of your Holy Guardian Angel.

Below are a list of questions which will help you become more honest with yourself. Please feel free to make up some questions of your own. However, we can not over emphasize the importance of answering these questions before you continue on to Chapter Eleven.

1. My basic beliefs about life are?
2. My perceived strengths are?
3. My perceived weaknesses are?
4. List the two best decisions I have made in my life.
5. List the two worst decisions I have made in my life.
6. What factors were present that helped me in my good decisions?
7. Examine the elements of critical thinking in my decisions that went awry and list them.
8. My desired personal and professional goals for the next year are?
9. My desired personal and professional goals for the next five years are?
10. My desired personal and professional goals for the next ten years are?
11. Are my stated personal goals congruent with my professional goals?
12. What is the thread of personal meaning that runs through all my goals?

13. Name a change I would like to make in my personal life.

14. List the beliefs that restrain me from making this change.

15. List the beliefs that drive me to make the change.

16. How might I unbalance these forces and drives so I might move out of the dark of conflict into the Light?

17. How do I spend money and how does it relate to my hopes, goals and dreams?

18. If I found a $1000.00 how would I spend the money—now?

19. Would my two closest associates and/or friends make the same decision?

20. How do I rate my ability to manage my personal finances? Excellent, Good, Fair, Poor.

21. How do I rate my ability to manage my time?

22. Am I more task, or more relationship focused. Or Both?

23. List the methods I use to help me carry out my plans, schedules, things to do, etc.

24. Add three to five questions of your own making including questions about your sexual experiences, traumas and joys.

Place this data in your journal.

Remember with this type of Operation you are setting in motion very powerful forces that will continue to provide further guidance and insight through dreams and events even after the Divination is closed.

After you have formed the general question you would have answered by or concerning your Holy Guardian Angel, pay close attention to your dreams and life events for further input and details of the question. Continue to expand your list.

After you have formulated the question and know what it specifically means to you, get a clean piece of white cardboard and print out your general question using your name and the three minor arcana symbols according to the following instructions.

In the center of the board print the title of your Personal Symbol (Small Card) using a Yellow felt tip pen. To the left of your Personal Symbol, print out your Preceding Personal Symbol with a Red felt tip pen. To the right of your Personal Symbol, print out your Progressive Personal Symbol with a Blue felt tip pen.

Underneath these three symbols write your name with a Black felt-tip pen.

Under your name print the question. Example; "What is my true Will or Destiny?"

Underneath the question, print out the name of your Character Symbol (Court Card), your Archetypal Symbol (Major Arcana Card), and the Card that best represents the day when you will be performing the Divination (Day Card). Your Archetypal card should be in the middle with the Character Card to the left and the "Day" Card to the right.

CREATION OF ENVIRONMENT

For at least three days prior to Divination perform the Banishing Ritual of the Pentagram and the Meditation of the Seer twice daily. (See Appendices.)

This should be performed in the presence of a New Deck of Symbols that you should have purchased for this particular situation. After you have performed the Banishing Ritual, you should begin to shuffle and handle the cards for at least 10 minutes, while you perform the Meditation of the Seer.

The new deck of symbols should be in your possession for at least one month. You should wrap them in something that holds great significance to you, along with the question written on a piece of paper. The symbols should be left unopened in their box, until you begin performing the Banishing Ritual. Prior to that time they should be in close proximity to where you sleep.

One week prior to the Divination, begin to purify yourself further with diet and light exercise. Slowly begin to remove all unnecessary and heavy foods from your diet. Fortify yourself with fresh food and water. Avoid, as much as possible, social distractions and idle conversations but it is not necessary to be a complete hermit.

THE DAY BEFORE

The day before the Divination should be spent as quietly as possible. Reduce your food intake, however, do not make yourself weak. Begin to cleanse your Divinatory environment of mundane symbols and messes. Disconnect your phone and darken the area were the Divination will be performed. Tell any friends that normally call that you will be busy.

Dress yourself in clean, loose fitting clothes. Bring to the environment anything you have that might have been empowered by yourself or someone you feel good about.

PREPARING THE LAYOUT

The layout used for this Divination is called the *Modified Tree of Life.*

Prior to beginning, prepare ten circles made of paper or poster board to represent each of the ten Sephiroth. Write the name of the Sephiroth (as you see below) and arrange them in order on your divining table. Use the Tree of Life diagram provided earlier in this book.

THE MEANINGS OF EACH POSITION

The First Position:
The Crown

Kether—The Crown: The Pinnacle, the Apex, the Prime Radiance of my Spirit.

The Crown is in fact the essence of your question in a complete yet undeveloped form.

I have known some people who have carried their symbol for this position with them for as long as a year to squeeze out the essence of its meanings in terms that they could consciously understand.

The Second Position:
The Father Who Must Wear The Crown

Chokmah—Wisdom, that which Enriches me.

This technically is the position of opposition. However, the word opposition is misleading. This symbol is simply the necessary counter force that when applied to first symbol allows us to consciously experience the process of evolution. However, the degree of consciousness of this position is minimal and frequently misunderstood. Since as humans we can only understand things from our own point of view, we require the model of conflict and opposition (yes/no) thinking in order to consciously understand and communicate events and experiences.

If you view the opposing force as an opposition you are taking the wrong path. It is simply the oxygen that the fire requires.

The Third Position:
The Mother Who Must Wear The Crown

Binah—Understanding, that which gives me Meaning, though sometimes through harshness.

This symbol represents the goal or the best possible outcome of the question. It is the result or resolution of the two *previous* forces at work. You must compare this symbol to the last symbol of the divination to understand its true significance.

The Fourth Position

Chesed—Mercy, that which brings Good-Will and Aid in my quest.

This position reflects your conscious attitude and or your emotional state regarding yourself and what has separated you from your Secret Lover. This position is that of the rich uncle in that your attitude toward your life or work can and does affect its outcome. Thus the rich uncle's gifts (attitude and emotional state) are powerful forces that must be used wisely. This symbol should make sense to you in relation to the dynamic interaction of the first two symbols.

The Fifth Position

Geburah—Severity, that which brings Turbulence and Adversity. Learning by trial.

This symbol reflects the forces or causes of the past that are now affecting the issue at hand.

The Sixth Position

Tiphareth—Beauty, that which is the Aura and Radiance I project.

This card reflects the Anahata Chakra and is the home of the Secret Lover. This is a most significant position and the card in this location will help you obtain the primary goal of all magical operations the direct and divine Knowledge and Conversation of your Holy Guardian Angel. *This card and the 10th card are the two key cards for working the Operations described in Chapter Eleven.*

The Seventh Position

Netzach—Victory, that which is my Achievement.

Relates to the conscious motive of the inquiry. This card can provide important clues into the troubles or difficulties that you are experiencing in your daily life as well as with the reading.

The Eighth Position

Hod—Glory, my Splendor and Distinction.

Represents the outside or environmental forces that are working on you and your question. This symbol can also be used to reflect dangers and help that might be coming from forces outside of your control.

The Ninth Position

Yesod—Foundation, that which is my Underpinning and Root.

This symbol predicts nothing, but instead shows what conscious or unconscious hopes (desires) or fears (unwanted desires) are operating.

This card helps you to determine the relationship between your desires and the reality of your circumstances. For example if this card is negative and the rest of the reading is strongly positive it indicates that you use negativity as a defense mechanism against disappointment. And, success or getting what you want also scares you. Remember for many people getting what they say they want is the worst thing that can happen to them.

The Tenth Position

Malkuth—Kingdom, that which is my Sphere and Realm. How it will manifest itself.

This symbol is the culmination of the reading, and is one of the key cards which leads you into the direction of your Secret Lover. In the ceremony of the Royal Mass this card becomes a talisman—an essential part of the power of the Eucharist ritual.

The empowerment of this symbol with the Eucharist opens a divine pathway to the Heart of the Secret Lover which is represented by position number Six.

This symbol and the sixth symbol coming down from Kether determine the pathways and byways into the source of all guidance and ecstasy.

THE BEGINNING

Perform the Banishing Ritual one hour before you start. Dress, bring in all your equipment and perform the Meditation of the Seer for at least 30 minutes. Now do the Middle Pillar Ritual. Banish one last time and Meditate on the Divine Name IAO (ee—ah—oh). This can be used as a temporary name for your Secret Lover until the Angel reveals its true name.

On top of your Divining location, place your Archetypal Symbol in the Middle, your Character Symbol to the right, and your Personal Symbol to the left.

Place the deck of symbols at the bottom of the Tree.

Place your empowered or sacred objects at the top of Tree, above the top Sephirah, Kether the Crown.

Darken the room and light a candle. If you wish at this time you may light an incense stick and put on some music that will elevate your mind and thoughts.

Pick up the cards. Shuffle and cut them for at least five minutes concentrating on your idea of your Holy Guardian Angel. When you feel the moment is right lay out the cards in a fan before you. Meditate on Ajna (the "third eye"), imagining that it is now opening. Select a card and place it face down on circle number one. Attempt to keep the image of the Third eye in your imagination throughout the entire Divination.

Now pick the second card and place it on the second circle. Continue until all ten symbols have been placed face down on the ten circles.

Allow enough light into the room so you can see each symbol.

Turn each card up one at a time. Do not interpret them. Look at each symbol for at least one minute.

After they are all face up look at the entire picture. Soak up the image. Let it permeate your entire mind.

Now relax for a few moments, take a few deep breaths. Go and get yourself a little food and drink. Stay away for 20-30 minutes. Just enjoy.

When you return, let yourself look at all the symbols. Write down any thoughts you have at this time. Your first impressions will be very helpful later as you explore the meanings of the symbols.

Carefully write down the symbols and their positions in your journal. Also, record the thoughts and feelings you experienced in the ensuing moments. These initial images are the first "whisperings" of your Holy Guardian Angel. At this point you may not understand the meanings of the cards in the various positions. In any event, you should not attempt to intellectually interpret the layout as if it were a fortune telling spread.

This process is only the first step in a far greater magical operation. You will ponder these living symbols for the rest of your life as they represent the day you impressed the universe with your will to achieve spiritual liberation.

CHAPTER TEN

THE WAY OF THE SECRET LOVER

I am the Heart; and the Snake is entwined
About the invisible core of the mind.
Rise, O my snake! It is now is the hour
of the hooded and holy ineffable flower.
Rise, O my Snake, into brilliance of bloom
On the corpse of Osiris afloat in the tomb!
O heart of my mother, my sister, mine own,
Thou art given to Nile, to the terror Typhon!
Ah me! but the glory of ravening storm
Enswathes thee and wraps thee in frenzy of form.
Be still, O my soul! that the spell may dissolve
As the wands are upraised, and the aeons revolve.
Behold! in my beauty how joyous Thou art,
O Snake that caresses the crown of mine heart!
Behold! we are one, and the tempest of years
Goes down to the dusk, and the Beetle appears.
O beetle! the drone of Thy dolorous note
Be ever the trance of this tremulous throat!
I await the awaking! The summons on high
From the Lord Adonai, from the Lord Adonai!
V.V.V.V.V.
Invocation of the Kundalini

On the Qabalistic diagram of the Tree of Life the
experience of union with the Secret Lover takes place
in the Sixth Sephirah, Tiphareth. This Sephirah corresponds directly to the Anahata (heart) Chakra. In
Hindu terms the Knowledge and Conversation of the
Holy Guardian Angel is the Kundalini energy raised to

117

the level of the heart Chakra. It is no coincidence that the cults of both Christ and Krishna encourage you to "give your heart" to their respective gods or refer to the deity as living *in,* opening *up* or coming *into* the hearts of the devotional.

י ה ו ה

As we learned in the chapter on the Qabalah, the formula of **YHVH** (**Yod Heh Vau Heh**) reveals both the secret of the descent of Spirit into Matter and the secret of humanity's return to Godhead.

ה

Each of us is the **Heh** (final) the Daughter/Princess in this Qabalistic family. In order to realize our original Divine nature we must first become one with:

ו

Vau the Son/Prince who is at the same time the brother and lover to the Princess.

*[At this time it is nearly useless for us to theorize on the nature of **Heh** the Mother and **Yod** the Father for until we are one with the **Vau** we will not have a sufficient capacity to comprehend the nature of these Supernals.]*

Heh has the numerical value of Five and is symbolized by the Pentagram. The five points of the Pentagram represent the Four Elements ruled by the fifth Element, Spirit. Five represents the Microcosm "the small world" whose ultimate expression is Man.

Vau has the numerical value of Six and is symbolized by the Hexagram. The six points of the Hexagram represent the Six Planets of the ancients surrounding the Sun which is found in the center of the Hexagram. Six represents the Macrocosm "the big world" which is the ultimate expression of God. Vau is also the special symbol of the Holy Guardian Angel.

The Great Work is the Union of the Five (You) and the Six (Your Holy Guardian Angel.)

Logic tells us that as everything in the universe is connected, there is really no separation between these two worlds at all. And it is true. The separation is illusory. Knowledge and Conversation of the Holy Guardian Angel is achieved when the individual's world of Five is harmonized and comes into perfect alignment with the world of Six. Consequently the first step of the Great Work is to perfect your world of Five by bringing the body, mind, senses and emotions into balance. Much of this is accomplished by exercises and meditations like the ones in Chapter Nine.

This sounds like a lot of work. You might feel that to master one's Self and one's environment before beginning the Great Work is almost like saying "in order to overcome your troubles you must first overcome your troubles." And in one respect that is exactly what we are saying. But even though practice and discipline will always be necessary to prepare yourself as a satisfactory vessel for the Angel, contact with the Angel will only be realized through the process of concentrated devotion and, when the magical opportunity presents itself, complete surrender.

Religious devotion does not seem to come as easily to Westerners as it does to our Eastern brothers and sisters. The semi-literate TV evangelists who terrorize their flocks into spiritual "surrender" exhibit the "dark side" of devotion by strictly defining the nature of their god and then demanding that the faithful flush intellect and common sense down the toilet. This is "surrender" at the point of a gun.

Is it any wonder that many intelligent seekers in the West have abandoned any hope of pursuing a Western path of devotion and have turned to Eastern religions to feed this natural spiritual hunger?

The Hindus call the spiritual science of devotion and surrender Bhakti Yoga and have devised countless techniques to bring the devotee into direct contact with the deity. Chanting the god's name, (the technique of the Hare Krishna movement), is one method. Pilgrimages to the god's holy city and shrines or performing acts and sacrifices that are traditionally pleasing to the deity are others.

To love with all your heart, the heart must first be opened. This is where the meeting takes place, the mysterious union between Man and God. In some mystical traditions, there is an expectation of rejection of the man below the belt. This attitude is not only found in some Christian mysticism, but also among the Jains. Israel Regardie, furthermore, has remarked about a similar split among followers of the Golden Dawn tradition. He discovered that they either over-indulge or act-out their sexuality and aggression, or repress it completely. Both extremes have produced as much *dis*-ease as they provided ease. The most serious criticism of this split, as I would see it, is a false view of man.

Man is not either/or, but both. Neither God nor beast are we, but both; not alone nor separate, but one; meeting in the heart as The Holy Guardian Angel.

With the experience of the Knowledge and Conversation the center of our focus changes. A switch is turned on; we are filled with the white light which bursts forth from the eternal darkness. The clouds disappear, and when they re-appear again we take only little notice. The mind is fixed in the heart, where the meeting of God and man is taking place. There is no room for anything else. The cup is overflowing and the fertilizing waters bring to life the dynamic interchange of Love and Will. I do not want to imply here that once this has taken place one lives continually in total bliss. Our mortality is such, that we always fall back into *dis*-ease and discord. We *require* this to evolve further. Once the deep union has taken place, however, there is the fundamental change in attitude, so that at least the memory remains, in the midst of our despairs and loneliness. We can thereby, from memory alone, embark once more on the search for that bliss of union that once experienced is never lost.

There are limitless ways of achieving the end desired, so far as external acts are concerned. The whole secret, however may be summed up in the words of Abraham the Jew: *"Enflame thyself in praying."*

THE FAIRY PRINCE

ADONAI! Thou inmost Fire
  Self-glittering image of my soul,
Strong lover to thy Bride's desire,
  Call me and claim me and control!
I pray Thee keep the holy tryst
Within this ring of Amethyst.

The above is the first verse of *The Invocation of the Ring* from Aleister Crowley's *The Wake World*. It is a fantasy story of a young girl and her marriage to her Fairy Prince who takes her step by step up the initiatory Tree of Life. This charming and ingenious tale, told in the images of the Tarot, is an excellent description of relationship with the Holy Guardian Angel as the Secret Lover and *The Invocation Of The Ring* is one of the most powerful enchantments ever written. It can and has been used with success as a sacred *mantra* to focus the mind and heart upon the Secret Lover.

In the story Lola (the young girl) is given an amethyst ring by her Fairy Prince who tells her she need only look into the Ring and say the poem and He will appear and take her on wonderful adventures. Each time he appears he kisses her. With each kiss she "awakens" to higher and higher states of consciousness. Eventually he will take Lola as his bride and make her Queen of his Palace.

He is called *Adonai*, a Hebrew word usually translated "Lord." Like IAO it has become the "generic" term for the Holy Guardian Angel but is replaced by the real name of one's own Angel once contact has been made and the name revealed.

Thou inmost Fire, indicates that the Holy Guardian Angel is the central life of each individual, not an alien being. *Self-glittering image of my soul* tells us that in reality the Angel is the radiant reflection of our innermost being—our self made perfect—more accurately it *is* our perfect self.

The ancient Egyptians referred to this self-glittering image as the Khabs which literally means star and is the innermost, essential Self of each individual. The light of this star is the L.V.X. of Western Hermeticism.

In *The Law is for All* (New Falcon Publications 1991) Aleister Crowley elucidates upon the Khabs;

> We are not to regard ourselves as base beings, without whose sphere is Light or "God." Our minds and bodies are veils of the Light within. The uninitiate is a "dark star," and the Great Work for him is to make his veils transparent by "purifying" them. This "purification" is really "simplification"; it is not that the veil is dirty, but that the complexity of its folds make it opaque. The Great Work therefore consists principally in the solution of complexes. Everything in itself is perfect, but when things are muddled they become "evil".

Regardless of the gender of the magician the Secret Lover "takes" you as a *Strong lover* "takes" a *Bride* who longs to be taken. These are the same roles assumed by the god Shiva and his Shakti in the Mahanirvana Tantra. In this case the Holy Guardian Angel of course is Shiva and you his Shakti. This in no way limits the sexual image or the spiritual "gender" of your Angel. It is entirely a matter of attitude. If you find it difficult to assume this attitude of complete surrender when devotionally invoking your Holy Guardian Angel you may wish to more deeply examine yourself and discover the reasons underlying this block.

WHAT SEX IS MY ANGEL?

It is often asked, what sex is the Holy Guardian Angel? The answer lies with each individual. The theoretical concept is that the Angel transcends gender but the fact remains each of us yearn for sexual union with other individuals who exhibit certain qualities that attract us. The Holy Guardian Angel will not necessarily have the same qualities you look for in a physical lover. In fact they may be quite different. One thing is for certain your Secret Lover is the most beautifully attractive Being you will ever encounter and you will fall instantly and eternally in love. The Angel will *call* to you and you will realize that you have heard that call forever but for some reason had ignored it. The pain of being separated even for instant is almost fatal. And when your Angel *claims* you and begins to *control* you in the dance of union all sense of male/female, top/bottom, Heaven/Earth in/out, front or back will vanish.

> *For on mine eyes the Sun*
>   *Hath dawned; my vigil slew the Night.*
> *I saw the image of the One:*
>   *I came from darkness into Light.*
> *I pray Thee keep the holy tryst*
> *Within this ring of Amethyst.*

As we mentioned earlier, the experience of the Knowledge and Conversation of the Holy Guardian Angel occurs in the Sixth Sephirah of Tree of Life, Tiphareth which corresponds to the *Sun* in the cosmic body of God. It is no coincidence that saints have universally referred to themselves as holding a *vigil* through the darkness of the *Night* and the experience of union as the *dawning* of a *Sun*.

If you refer to the diagram of the Tree of Life you will see that Tiphareth is a direct reflection of the First Sephirah, Kether. It is from Tiphareth that the magician can first see *the image of the One*.

> *I.N.R.I.—me crucified,*
>   *Me slain, interred, arisen, inspire!*
> *T.A.R.O.—me glorified,*
>   *Anointed, fill with frenzied Fire!*
> *I pray Thee keep the holy tryst*

Within this ring of Amethyst.

This verse refers to the Golden Dawn initiation ceremony for the Grade of Adeptus Minor (5=6) which corresponds to Tiphareth. (Counting from the bottom of the Tree of Life Tiphareth is the fifth Sephirah, counting from the top it is the sixth.) In this ritual the candidate is ceremonially crucified. Later he or she is taken to the tomb of the mythical Christian Rosenkreutz where with the help of the candidate the ancient Master is gloriously resurrected.

Among the secrets of this degree (which is symbolic of the Knowledge and Conversation of the Holy Guardian Angel) are the Signs of the Hidden Wisdom of the Order. I.N.R.I. These are identical with the signs used in the Hexagram Ritual. As mentioned above, the Hexagram is the symbol of the Holy Guardian Angel and the ritual of the Hexagram operates upon the Macrocosm.

Traditionally the Latin letters I.N.R.I. appear written on a scroll and nailed above the head of the crucified Christ. The exoteric explanation is that these are the initials of the sentence; *Jesus Nazaranus Rex Judaeorum.* (Jesus the Nazarene, King of the Jews).

The Qabalistic analysis of the letters I.N.R.I. reveals the formula of Creation, Destruction and Resurrection that was represented by the pre-Christian Gnostics by the name of God, IAO.

I.N.R.I. = ʼ Yod ב Nun ר Resh ʼ Yod.

ʼ = Virgo, Isis, Mighty Mother

ב = Scorpio, Apophis, Destroyer.

ר = Sol, Osiris, Slain and Risen.

ʼ = the Mighty Mother is resurrected *as* Osiris

Isis, Apophis, Osiris = **IAO.**

This verse of the poem also indicates that in any formal ceremonial invocation of the Holy Guardian Angel that it is appropriate to incorporate the formula of the Hexagram. An example of such a ceremony can be found in Chapter Eleven and the Hexagram Ritual will be found in Appendix Six.

> *I eat my flesh: I drink my blood*
> *I gird my loins: I journey far:*
> *For thou hast shown the Rose, the Rood*
> *The Eye, the Sword, the Silver Star.*
> *I pray Thee keep the holy tryst*
> *Within this ring of Amethyst.*

In this verse we move from the subjective, *mystical* images to objective *magical* practices, in particular the Eucharist.

> One of the simplest and most complete of Magick ceremonies is the Eucharist.
>   It consists in taking common things, transmuting them into things divine, and consuming them...
>   ...Take a substance (This may be of a composite character.) symbolic of the whole course of nature, make it God and consume it.   — *Aleister Crowley*

Almost everyone is familiar with some form of Eucharistic ceremony. In the Ancient Mithraic mysteries the candidate, after bathing in the blood of the sacrificial bull, ceremonially drank its blood and ate of its flesh. By doing so the Deity became part of the flesh and blood of the candidate who had become a new, semi-divine individual by having partaken of the God.

The wine and bread of the Christian tradition are anemic shadows of such primitive Eucharists but nonetheless the idea has the potential of great power.

In truth the physical elements of the Eucharist (the blood and flesh of the bull or the bread and wine of the Mass) are merely symbolic objects, talismans. Moreover, any magical power or spiritual virtue they may contain is derived exclusively from the individual or individuals responsible for "charging" them.

It follows that the most efficacious *flesh* and *blood* for the elements of the Eucharist would actually be part of (or come from) one's own self.

> *Prostrate I wait upon Thy will,*
> *Mine Angel, for this grace of union.*
> *O let this Sacrament distill*
> *Thy conversation and communion.*
> *I pray Thee keep the holy tryst*
> *Within this ring of Amethyst.*

With this passionate last verse the devotee awaits the Angel in an attitude of absolute surrender. Undisguised, the Secret Lover takes his Bride. Once united, their ecstasy transforms them both and in the Light of their metamorphosis an elixir forms like dew. No longer a Princess, the new Queen gathers this dew and brings it to her Lover who is now King. Together they share what was once their essence but is now greater then sum of both their essences and the communion is complete.

CHAPTER ELEVEN

THE ROYAL MASS
OF THE SECRET LOVER

(Note: This operation is Also Known As The Royal Mass of the Vault. This is used by Most High and Secret Initiates prior to Temple Initiation in the Grade of Adeptus Minor. It is done in private, prior to the Most Sacred Temple Operations. The alchemical process here will be immediately recognized by those students of the Vault of the Adepti).

Thoth says unto him: *"Who is He whose Pylons are of Flame, whose walls of Living Uraei, and the flames of whose House are streams of Water?"*
And the Initiate replies: *"Osiris!"*
And it is immediately proclaimed: *"Thy meat shall be of the Infinite, and thy drink from the Infinite. Thou art able to go forth to the sepulchral feast on earth, for thou hast overcome."*

INITIATION & THE SECRET LOVER

Three days prior to this operation the couple or individual must have performed the Ultimate Divination. No intercourse or sexual play should be engaged in between completing the Ultimate Divination and the Operation of the Secret Lover.

A full day should be set aside for this operation. The Sanctuary of the Royal Gnosis should be prepared the first thing in the Morning. It is advisable to have every-

129

thing as new and clean as possible prior to performing this ceremony.

A day should be chosen which best represents the qualities and aspirations of the individual or couple. This can be done by simply looking at an ephemeris or by meditation.

For this operation the couple or individual shall have performed the Banishing Ritual of the Pentagram and the Middle Pillar (see Appendices) in the Sanctuary. Remember, do not concern yourselves with the results of this operation. Now is not the time.

THE OATH

I (We) Dedicate this work to my (Our) Secret Lover who is my (Our) Holy Guardian Angel.

The experience of direct divine knowledge and conversation of the Secret Lover can happen at any time during or after the performance of these operations.

This work may be performed individually or by a couple. We will discuss this most Royal Union as if it were performed by a heterosexual couple. Let this form of discussion give no impression other than the authors are most familiar with this form of operation.

While the direct knowledge and conversation can and will be obtained by a single individual there are very specific advantages which can only be obtained by a couple. The reason for this is simple. Each partner has a Secret Lover. Thus, the four letters of Tetragrammaton are duly represented; we have the Father, Mother, Son and Daughter. The act of two has created the entire dynamic principle of the universe. Historically this aspect of the operation has been one of the best guarded secrets of the Adepts.

THE MARITAL VOW

Dearly beloved, (I or We) have come into the sight of Isis and Osiris having duly performed the necessary rituals prior to our mystical union. We have adorned and beautified our presence and this Sanctuary of the Royal Gnosis with incense, light and color. We have removed all dross from our minds and hearts and openly present ourselves, as children of light, to partake of the Eucharist which is a symbol of Divine radiance.

We charge ourselves with the secrets of the heart and sanctify this marriage with the Eucharist of our True Will.

I _____ a child of light take this opportunity to cast aside the garments of darkness and take on the garments of light.

I _____ a child of light take this opportunity to cast aside the garments of darkness and take on the garments of light.

Both individuals should sign this document which represents their intent and freedom in taking this action.

Each person should then repeat out loud:

> In the presence of the Lords of the Universe I affix my signature as a sign that it is my True Will to undertake this most holy operation of the Secret Lover.

The couple should embrace and then give the sign of Shu. (See Appendix Four.)

Both should now say this:

> Bless us, O Holy Lords, with the holy sacrament of direct and divine knowledge and conversation of our

Secret Lover and may we dedicate this work and all
that shall come of it to thy Holy Presence.

FIRST OPERATION

Now, the male shall be stimulated by the female a
minimum of eleven times until his organ becomes his
wand of inspiration. The male shall stimulate the
female until her veil opens and the lustral waters of
heaven pour forth.

When this is accomplished the female shall mount
the male (if this be the most comfortable position). The
goal of this first meeting is to exchange glances, touch
the hearts, and share the first distillate of Holy
Eucharist. Thus, this is a brief operation. The male and
female shall not attempt to control themselves. They
shall simply move as dramatically and dynamically as
possible, with each movement, breathing deeply and
loudly. With each breath the mind should imagine the
power of the Universe entering the anus and exiting
through the anus. They should partake in the Eucharist
of their creation, then bathe and rest.

SECOND OPERATION

An hour should pass between the first operation and
the second operation.

The Tarot symbol from the position of Malkuth
obtained in the Ultimate Divination should be brought
into the Sanctuary of the Royal Gnosis.

This image, regardless of its nature, shall be focused
upon until the eyes begin to tire. The symbol should
then be placed in a secret and dark place. It shall act as
a talisman which shall partake in the Holy Eucharist of
this operation.

Later when the talisman has been consecrated with the Eucharist of the Royal Love it shall be placed in a darker and deeper place were it shall gestate and transmute for a period of one year, until the anniversary of this divine operation.

The date of this operation shall become as a Holy Day for the operants. Every year this day shall be celebrated as if it were a Birth.

Once the meditation is complete and the Tarot symbol first hidden, the couple shall regain the forces of Love through mutual stimulation. It does not matter how this is accomplished.

When the gates of the veil have been penetrated again by the wand of inspiration and the waters of heaven have lustrated this holy union, let the couple begin deep breathing, imagining that the forces of the Universe are entering the anus and exiting through the genitals.

Now this is very important. It is not simply air which one is imagining, it is the Light of the Stars of Creation itself, which enters the Anus and exits the genitals.

Thus, with each genital stroke the Holy Light of the Universe is entering the bodies and souls of the celebrants and the most profound magical exchange takes place.

This operation must be done very slowly. This is sometimes referred to as *slow heat*. At least 15 minutes should be spent in this act, so a comfortable position should be chosen.

Now, the couple shall begin to focus on the image of the Tarot symbol. This should be done in the place of Ajna (the third eye). With each breath imagine the light of the Universe entering the enjoined genitals penetrat-

133

ing the image at Ajna, soaking it with divine light. This should be continued for at least 10 minutes.

The couple then should drop all meditations and begin to wildly make love reaching orgasm as quickly as possible. Exhausted and before sleep ensues, the second distillate of the Eucharist should be shared with a drop of it placed upon the Tarot card in operation. The Tarot Card should now be hidden for the second and last time. The couple should then sleep or rest for at least two hours. Small amounts of food and alcohol may now be consumed. These should have been prepared ahead of time and if possible should have been kept in the Sanctuary.

THE THIRD & SUPREME OPERATION

The Tarot symbol found in the place of Tiphareth during the Ultimate Divination shall be brought into the Sanctuary of the Royal Gnosis. It should be wrapped in a White cloth symbolizing the Holiness of the operation. The couple shall meditate upon until their eyes tire.

In this third and final operation the most divine astral nerve centers shall be stimulated. The location of work here is the Anahata (Heart) Chakra, also, known as Tiphareth in the tradition of Western Magic.

Here is the center of Divine Harmony and the Home of the Secret Lover. It can be symbolized by Osiris, Helios, Eros or Mithra and is the goal of all true Magical operations. Its location on the Tree of Life is between Kether and Yesod, thus all psycho-spiritual centers of the Middle Pillar must be stimulated.

The location of Tiphareth is the point of Union were the forces of the microcosm and macrocosm unite. It is symbolized by the Hexagram and by a point in the center of the Hexagram.

Unlike some magical or mystical operations which take place *only* in the Imagination, this final operation takes place in the Imagination, the body and the soul of the aspirant. This union of Imagination and Body is completely in adherence with the goal of all True Western Magical Operations as demonstrated by the most ancient and powerful initiations and alchemies.

The couple should jointly perform the Banishing Rituals of the Pentagram and the Hexagram (refer to the Appendices).

The following prayer should be said jointly. As the couple repeats the prayer let them "enflame" themselves with the power of Love.

> I am Toom, the Setting Sun, I am the only being in the firmament of Heaven.
>
> I am Ra, the Rising Sun, I have passed from the Gate of Death unto Life.
>
> The Sun's power beginneth again after he hath set; he riseth again (so doth the justified Spirit of Man.)
>
> I am the Great God begotten of himself; I can never be turned back by the Elementary Powers; I am the Morning, I Know the Gate. (I ever rise again unto existence. I know the pathway through death unto life.)
>
> The Father of the Spirit; the Eternal Soul of the Sun. He hath examined and He hath proved me. He hath found that I fought on Earth the battle of the good Gods, as He, my Father, Lord of the Invisible World ordered me to do.
>
> I know the Great God who existeth in the Invisible.
>
> I am the Great Phoenix which is in Annu, the former of my Life and my Being am I.

In order to activate the correct image of the entire Tree of Life which includes the pillars of Severity and Mercy symbolized by the Crook and Scourge of Osiris the following should be read a day or two before the operation.

Thus, while you symbolize the Middle Pillar, you have neatly placed in your subconscious the Pillars of Severity and Mercy to be activated when and where they wish in this most Sacred Sanctuary of the Royal Gnosis.

THE IMAGE TO BE PLACED IN THE MIND

Once the "Soul" has passed through the ordeal (refers to death, judgment, etc.) it is "...then introduced into the Presence of Osiris by Horus. Osiris sits in his Shrine upon a throne, with the Crook and Scourge, symbols of Mercy and Severity in his hands; behind him are Isis and Nephthys, the Goddesses of Nature and Perfection; and before him are the four Genii of the Dead upon the Lotus Flower, the emblem of the Metempsychosis. Thus the whole of the Symbols upon the pillars represent the advance and purification of the Soul, and its uniting with Osiris the Redeemer; in that Golden Dawn of an Infinite Light wherein the soul is transfigured; knows all and can do all; for it hath become joined unto Eternal Gods."

The wand of power and the veil (Gate) of the Sanctuary should be brought into operation. It is of the utmost importance that the couple be fortified for this operation as it must exhaust them. They are coupling their will and desire for direct and divine knowledge and communication with the Holy Guardian Angel, "against" the desire of the body to give in—let go—

and "die" at its will. Thus, they are creating an intense spiritual heat.

Thus, this act the charging the Eucharist is created by the eternal process of birth, death and resurrection and is fully symbolized and enacted by complete Surrender.

The couple should choose a position which allows the altar (the bed) to support them.

When they have joined they should begin breathing taking first in the Light through the anus and allowing it to flow through and out of the Anahata. This should be done for 10 minutes. Remember with each slow rhythmic breath the wand and the veil should be slowly stimulated by movement.

Next they should allow the Light of the Universe to flow through Sahasrara, the lotus of the thousand petals, the Chakra positioned directly above the head, the home of Amoun and Ptah. The Light should flow out of Anahata, the home of the Secret Lover. This should be done for 10 minutes.

Next, the Light of the Universe should emerge from the genitals, the home of Shu, and flow through Anahata. This should be done for 10 minutes.

Finally, the Light of the Universe should emerge *from* Anahata and flow *through* Anahata. This should be done for 10 minutes.

(Note: The invisible Sephira Daath has been deliberately left out in this operation; those familiar with it and its holy name may use it.)

When this is completed the couple should wildly and passionately make love surrendering themselves to the Ecstasy of the Secret Lover. Upon satisfaction, the third distillate Eucharist should be shared. The couple should be quiet being open to the presence of the All.

This moment has been called by the Wise—The Epiphany.

Later, the Tarot symbol from the location of Tiphareth should be adored and anointed with the Elixir. This symbol should be also hidden and left undisturbed for one year.

The Sanctuary of the Royal Gnosis should be closed with the Banishing Ritual of the Pentagram.

This is then the act of establishing Direct and Divine Knowledge and Conversation of the Holy Guardian Angel. Practice this ritual as often as necessary to assure that a deep and everlasting contact is made. The Epiphany will lengthen and increase in intensity with practice.

The energies of Love feed the relationship and the Secret Lover will satisfy itself with the joy that it will take in you.

Your Secret Lover will be your Lover and your guide throughout your engagement on this planet, as well as your guide in the afterlife.

CHAPTER TWELVE

THE MYSTICAL/MAGICKAL MEANING
OF THE ROYAL MASS

The Royal Mass is the synthesis of many complicated and complex magical operations. Some have said that within it lay the quintessence of all that Man yearns for in this life.

While the Mass is a magickal operation, its goal is purely "mystical" (if we mean by that term union with the Divine). More, the Royal Mass is both transpersonal as well as personal. Thus, the Mass meets the requirements of Magick, Mysticism and strangely enough, psychosexuality. The last point stems from the openness and emotional depth of the Royal Mass which requires of the couple a love and a freedom unknown in normal sexuality, which is overburdened by guilt, obsession and shrouded with obligations.

(1) The magickal tone of the operation is in the various rituals and the making of talismans. Unlike most talismans which have a quality of deadness about them, those made from the Royal Mass are charged with the power and joy of the Universe; thus they are alive with the force of growth and infinite possibility.

(2) The mystical tone of the Royal Mass is in the invocation of the Holy Guardian Angel who becomes the Lover of the participant. Thus the requirement of surrender, which most mystics clamor about but rarely have an idea how to reach, is legitimately met.

Even at this point the Royal Mass meets the Supreme goal dreamed of by aspirants from the beginning of time. Individuality is absorbed into the infinite and maintained separately, fulfilling the obvious requirement that the Universe has set the stage for both Individuality and Union. The Universe demands both Ego and Non-Ego and any attempt to pass one as the other will mean complete defeat in this operation.

The fact that the operators start and direct the process and then surrender to their own creation only to find something more shows the utmost respect for "Ego and Non-Ego." There is no either/or here, the curse of the average religionist.

(3) The psychosexual component can best be appreciated in the context of the "normal" human relationship which can best be understood by what is missing from it: everything.

As a one-time psychotherapist, I abandoned psychotherapy when it finally struck me that very little true healing could occur within the context of legislated mental health. I was limited to activities analogous to that of a Doctor fixing a broken leg—which, of course, is very important for the man in pain. I came to the realization that the repaired leg might even be better than it was before, but still a "leg is not a wing."

Thus, when properly performed the Royal Mass transforms the psychosexual component of life making it more than ever imagined.

THE FORMULA OF YHVH

In this most sacred and powerful Magickal act the Supreme force is Love; Love under Will.

The lustral waters and the blood of life mingle in a Thunderous embrace, each mixing and renewing the earth with life. All necessary divisions come to an end in the frenzied excitement of the moment. The YH (Yod, Heh), the Father and Mother become VH (Vau, Heh(f)), the Prince and the Princess who then become the Father and Mother again. The couple transform into the ultimate magical weapon—the Cup and the Wand united—the Cucurbite—the crystal jeweled vessel—and the Athanor (the divine furnace). The substance created from this alchemical marriage, the Celestial Dew, becomes the Eucharist of the Communion. And within this entire process a new lover emerges—The Secret Lover (the Holy Guardian Angel.)

For the first time we see true love, equal and diverse, a cooperation for the benefit of all without an external moral commandment to assure and monitor its success. No one loses. (No doubt something must be wrong here—doesn't someone always have to lose?)

Power, Love, Self Mastery, Surrender, Ego, Non Ego, the Sun and the Moon, these are the results of the Royal Mass. Love under Will.

CHAPTER THIRTEEN

SONGS OF THE SECRET LOVER

Below are the songs of the Secret Lover as taken from the Song of Songs attributed to King Solomon.

These songs of love may be used by the Celestial bride and groom when performing the Royal Mass in Chapter Eleven.

It is important to keep in mind the relationship between the Bride and Groom and their God. There is no separation between love, sex and religion except in the minds of the profane.

The Bride:

Let him kiss me with the kisses of his mouth.
Your love is more delightful than wine;
delicate is the fragrance of your perfume,
your name is an oil poured out,
and that is why the maidens love you.
Draw in your footsteps, let us run.
The King has brought me into his rooms;
you will be our joy and our gladness.
We shall praise your love above wine;
how right it is to love you.

The Bridegroom:

How beautiful are your feet in their sandals,
O prince's daughter!
The curve of your thighs is like the curve of a necklace,

work of a master hand.
Your navel is bowl well rounded
with no lack of wine,
your belly a heap of wheat
surrounded with lilies.
Your two breasts are two fawns,
twins of a gazelle.
Your neck is an ivory tower.
Your eyes, the pools of Heshbon,
by the gate of Beth-rabbim.
Your nose, the Tower of Lebanon,
sentinel facing Damascus.
Your head is held high like Carmel,
and its plaits are as dark as purple;
a king is held captive in your tresses.
How beautiful you are, how charming,
my love, my delight!
In stature like the palm tree,
its fruit clusters your breasts.
'I will climb the palm tree,' I resolved,
'I will seize its clusters of dates.'
May be your breasts be clusters of grapes,
your breath sweet-scented as apples,
your speaking, superlative wine.

The Bride:

I sleep, but my heart is awake.
I hear my beloved knocking.
'Open to me, my sister, my love,
my dove, my perfect one,
for my head is covered with dew,
my locks with the drops of night.'
— 'I have taken off my tunic,
am I to put it on again?

144

I have washed my feet,
am I to dirty them again?'
My Beloved thrust his hand
through the hole in the door;
I trembled to the core of my being.
Then I rose
to open to my Beloved,
myrrh ran off my hands,
pure myrrh off my fingers,
on to the handle of the bolt.

The Bridegroom:

I awakened you under the apple tree,
there where your mother conceived you,
there where she who gave birth to you conceived you.
Set me like a seal on you heart,
like a seal on your arm.
For love is strong as Death,
jealousy relentless as Sheol.
The flash of it is a flash of fire,
a flame of YHVH himself.
Love no flood can quench,
no torrents drown.

CHAPTER FOURTEEN

THE CEREMONY OF
THE SUN AND MOON

Being a Ritual of Marriage designed for the Conjoining
of two souls in Nuit and Hadit.

Official Ceremony of the
Novus Ordo Aureae Aurora

by David Cherubim

Do what thou wilt shall be the whole of the Law.

I
THE ARRANGEMENT OF THE TEMPLE

The Temple shall be arranged accordingly: In the centre shall be the Altar, having upon it a Cup of Wine, two Cakes of Light, the Magick Wand, the Magick Bell, the Holy Oil, two Magical Links for the Priest and the Priestess (two consecrated Rings), and The Book of the Law.

II
THE PREPARATION OF THE CEREMONY

The Priest shall wear a Red (or White) Robe and the Priestess shall wear a Blue (or Black) Robe to symbolize Fire and Water (or Light and Darkness, that is, Male and Female). The Priest shall wear a Lamen of the Sun and the Priestess shall wear a Lamen of the

Moon. They shall duly purify their bodies before they robe.

To begin this Holy Ceremony of the Sun and Moon, let the Priest duly banish in the Temple by the proper magical method. (Perform the Banishing Ritual of the Star Ruby, Liber XXV). Then shall he apply the Holy Oil to himself and the Priestess shall do the same to herself, consecrating their Wills to this Great Work of Union. Then shall they kiss, uniting hands as they do so. Then shall they position themselves in their stations in the Temple, the Priest in the East of the Temple and the Priestess in the West, facing each other.

Before conducting this Holy Ceremony, the Priest and the Priestess should meditate in their hearts upon verses 33 and 34 of Chapter I and verse 35 of Chapter II of *The Book of the Law*. Let them perform this Holy Ceremony in accordance with these holy injunctions of Thelema. They should especially meditate upon and put into proper effect the holy injunction: "the rituals shall be half known and half concealed:"

III
THE PROCLAMATION AND THE OATH

Priest: (In the East facing Priestess in the West)
            Do what thou wilt shall be the whole of the Law.
Priestess: (In the West facing Priest in the East)
            Love is the law, love under will.
Priest: What is thy Will, O Lady of the Night?
Priestess: It is my Will to sacramentally Unite.
            And what is thy Will, O Man of the Sun?
Priest: It is my Will to become as One.
Priestess: And by what Magick Spell shall we work our Will?

Priest: By the Spell of this Ritual's Mystick Seal.
Priestess: And what shall we make by this act
              Unknown?
Priest: A mysterious object called the Philosopher's
              Stone!
Priestess: Art thou prepared to do thy Will?
Priest: I am prepared to accomplish the Grand
              Miracle.
Priestess: Will you take an Oath to complete this
              Rite?
Priest: I will take the Oath and we will Unite.
Priestess: Then seal thy words with a precious Kiss
              And so shall we unite in infinite Bliss!

The Priest and Priestess go to the Altar and the Priest kisses his Priestess on her lips. Then shall they unite hands above *The Book of the Law* on the Holy Altar, and together they shall take the Oath.

Priest and Priestess:

In freedom we take this Oath of love
To accomplish our Will on earth as above!
We promise and swear, and infinitely aspire,
To unite as one—our hearts desire!
By Fire and Water we will partake this hour
The Holy Sacrament of Magick Power!
And so shall we work our Will to Unite
And attain the Quintessence of the Rite!
This Oath we promise; this Oath we swear
As we enflame ourselves with Prayer!
In the Name of Thelema—the Law of Liberty,
As we will, So mote it be!

IV
THE INVOCATION OF THE ELEMENTS

The Priest advances to the appropriate Elemental quarters and invokes the Elements by way of the Unicursal Hexagram and the appropriate verbal invocations.

(Priest advances to the East, traces the Unicursal Hexagram of Earth, and invokes:)

> Holy art Thou, O Lord of the Earth,
> Thou Lord of Life, our essence of birth!
> O thou soul of all forms that we see,
> Come Thou forth we say unto Thee!

(Priest goes to the South, traces the Unicursal Hexagram of Fire, and invokes:)

> Holy art Thou, O Lord of the Fire,
> Thou Lord of Light, to which we aspire!
> O Thou Flashing Flame of Eternity,
> Come Thou forth we say unto Thee!

(Priest goes to the West, traces the Unicursal Hexagram of Water, and invokes:)

> Holy art Thou, O Lord of the Water,
> Thou Lord of Love and Mystick Rapture!
> O Thou inscrutable Depth of the Sea,
> Come Thou forth we say unto Thee!

(Priest goes to the North, traces the Unicursal Hexagram of Air, and invokes:)

> Holy art Thou, O Lord of the Air,
> Thou Lord of Liberty, to which we adhere!

O Thou perpetual Breath of Ecstasy,
Come Thou forth we say unto Thee!

(The Priest now goes to the Centre of the Temple, completing the Circle. He then gives the Sign of the Cross, and declares:)

Holy art thou, ye Elements Divine,
Invoked and inspired to perfectly combine
In this Temple consecrated to Love
To accomplish below That which is Above!

V
THE INVOCATION OF THE SUN AND MOON

The Priest and Priestess now exchange stations, so that the Priest is facing East and the Priestess is facing West.

Priest: (Makes Unicursal Hexagram of Sol, and invokes:)

I Invoke Thee, O Thou Glorious Sun,
To come Thou forth that our Will be done!
Let Thy Light illumine this Temple
Making true the Magick of this Holy Ritual!

Priestess: (Makes Unicursal Hexagram of Luna, and invokes:)

I invoke Thee, O Thou Soul of Night,
To come Thou forth that we may Unite!
Let Thy Love work its Mighty Spell
To make as one, both Heaven and Hell!

VI
THE CONJOINING OF THE SUN AND MOON

The Priest and Priestess shall now unite to produce the Philosopher's Stone, that they may duly charge their

Magical Links with the invoked Current of this Sacramental Ceremony of Love for the accomplishment of their Will to Unite. When this is complete, let the Priest consume the Elixir and administer the same unto his Priestess.

VII
THE CHARGING OF THE MAGICAL LINKS

A portion of the Philosopher's Stone shall be used to charge the Magical Links which are designed to bring about the desired magical effect of this Holy Ceremony. They shall be imbued with the invoked force of the Stone These links should be in the form of consecrated Magical Rings which shall be worn by the Priest and Priestess as true tokens of their consummation of this Sacramental Ceremony. The Priest shall do best by tracing the Sigil of the Moon on the Ring which he will administer to his Priestess, and the Priestess shall do best by tracing the Sigil of the Sun on the Ring which she will administer to her Priest.

Priest: (When tracing Sigil of Luna, let him declare:)

This ring I bless to unite my soul
With the Priestess of this Holy Ritual!

The Priest shall now kiss the Ring and place it on the proper finger of his Priestess.

Priestess (When tracing Sigil of Sol, let her declare:)

This ring I bless to unite my soul
With the High Priest of this Holy Temple!

VIII
THE PROCLAMATION OF
THE RINGS OF POWER

Both: Upon our fingers there is Magick Power,
          Rings of a Spell, by which we empower
          Our Will to unite in Love and Liberty—
          A Mystic delight for all eternity!
          These Rings of Love we do proclaim
          As Links of a Power we do acclaim!
          By their Magick we enforce our Way
          To work our Will both Night and Day!

IX
THE PROCLAMATION OF THE UNION
OF THE SUN AND MOON

Both: This we proclaim: that we are Bound
          In Mystick Love and Freedom Profound!
          Our divided souls are wed in Ecstasy:
          We are ever joined in Love and Liberty!

          This we Proclaim; that we are One:
          In the Sun and Moon our Will is Done!
          We shall now celebrate with Wine and
          Cake
          This blessed Union which we undertake!

X
THE CELEBRATION OF THE SUN AND MOON

Both: We partake the Cake; we partake the Wine:
          The bread and the blood—sacraments
          divine!

Let the Priest and the Priestess now partake the Cakes
and the Wine. When this is duly accomplished, they
shall then declare:

153

Both: We revel with joy in this act of Zeal,
          Partaking the elements with Love under
          Will.

The Priest and Priestess shall now embrace their bodies in pure passionate ecstasy and joy, ending all with a sacramental kiss of delicious delight as a final token of their Mystick Love.

XI
THE GREAT WORK ACCOMPLISHED

The Priest and Priestess shall now strike the Magick Bell. The Priestess shall hold the Bell on High, and the Priest shall strike the Bell 3-5-3 with his Wand. When this is duly accomplished, they then both proclaim:

ABRAHADABRA!

This final Word of Power seals this Sacramental Ceremony of Love with the Magical Current of the Great Work of Thelema, of which it is a proper magical glyph, being the glyph of the Magick Formula of the Mystick Union of the Rose and Cross. It is the Great Reward of Our Lord Ra-Hoor-Khuit, administered unto them who are chosen and united in Nuit and Hadit.

To properly end this Holy Ceremony, the Priest shall duly perform the Banishing Ritual of the Star Ruby (Liber XXV). Then shall the Priest and Priestess depart the Temple in unison, with hands joined to symbolize their going forth together to do their Will among the legions of the living; yea, to do their Will among the legions of the living.

Love is the law, love under will.

CHAPTER FIFTEEN

SEXUAL MAGIC: A CHAOS PERSPECTIVE

By Phil Hine

To begin with, a few definitions:

> — *"The Sex Magician attempts to integrate passion with consciousness."*

> — *"Sex Magick is Love under the direction of Will."*

Both of these definitions have been taken from the work of Dr. Christopher S. Hyatt, who combines magical practice with psychotherapeutic and bodywork techniques.

> — *"the harnessing of one's own sexual experience with intentionality, to bring about willed change."*

This third definition is an early attempt of mine to encapsulate the essential features of sexual magic. All three definitions though, place an emphasis on the Will. Dr. Hyatt stresses the importance of Love and Passion, whereas I have cast the net much wider to all aspects of one's sexual experience. So, to summarize from this point, sexual magic is about exploring and utilizing one's awareness and experience of sexuality in order to bring about change, in accordance with will. It does help, if you are able to be passionate, in all senses of the word, about this process, and without Love, it is difficult to change.

This implies a great deal more than the waving about of rods, wands, cups and roses that some occult writers drop hints about. The decision to be celibate for a while could be as much an act of sexual magic as any ritualized copulation or act of masturbation. There is a tendency among modern magicians to view sexual magic as just a 'more powerful' means of entering trance (gnosis) in order to bring about change. This is rather, as Zachary Cox put in *Aquarian Arrow* 22, like "...using a microcomputer as a doorstop."

Also, it's too easy to get stuck with a narrow, or limited impression of what sexual magic involves. One of the most intense invocations of 'erotic tension' I ever participated in took place across a crowded room full of partying people. It started with glances thrown across the room. We held each other's gaze for longer bursts. This 'dance' of non-verbal cues progressed slowly, with studied postural shifts, vocal underlining of significant words, a not-quite-touching of fingers until the erotic tension in the room began to heighten, until most people cottoned on, one way or another, that an atmosphere was building up, and so they left. Between us, we 'raised' an intense erotic ambiance, and created a 'highly charged' atmosphere, without anything overtly sexual happening. Since we had both shared the same lover in the past (unknown to anyone else in the room) we could do this as a playful game, acknowledging each other's seductive power but comfortable in the knowledge that we didn't want to ball each other. This to me, is as much an act of sexual magic as fiercely copulating while reciting a mantra or concentrating on a sigil.

Sex is powerful and dangerous. One of the most intimate aspects of human experience, yet, like an unskilled equestrian on a rather skittish horse, we often feel that our sexuality can suddenly slip from our control and carry us, gasping, into the chaos of the unfamiliar. Sexuality can be, at times, as slippery as an eel—just when we think we've grabbed it and understood it, it twists and surprises us. Sexuality is chaotic, therefore, in a way that few people want to admit. Western culture, after all, is obsessed with order—linear experience and everything neatly labeled. But it is nature, including our own inner natures of course, which is messy and blobby at the edges. Our sexuality can, seemingly at a moment's notice, come bubbling out of the limitations into which we try and contain it—the social institutions, gender-preferences, and psychological theories. Let's face it, Sexuality is *weird*. Magic is *weird*. So when you start in on Sexual Magic, you're in for a double helping.

Sex and magic are intertwined experiences—sex is one kind of magic (and can be made more *magical* without being concerned with sex-magic at any point), and magic can be, while erotic and arousing, not necessarily sexual in the way that is often understood. There is a commonly-held belief that those who practice sex-magic are indulging themselves in wild orgiastic rites at every opportunity. This is rarely the case. After all, if you need to go through lots of occult rigmarole just to get laid, then you're a bit sad, aren't you? Then again, the occult subculture is full of SAD people, desperate to finally get laid and attempting to turn to sex-magic as a last resort.

In this latter half of the twentieth century, there is a growing interest in sexual magic. This has both positive and negative consequences. Yes, a renewed interest in sexual magic means that there is a new generation of books and writers, moving beyond the old clichés and exploring taboos, but it also means that sex-magic becomes something of a *trend*, and trends tend to become, at some point, trivialized. Esoteric disciplines get boiled down into a weekend workshop. Everything gets the label "Shamanic"—transvestites are 'shamans', leather queens are 'shamans', anyone with more than one body piercing is "shamanic"—until the term "shaman" is stripped of meaning, and worse, people begin to think that all they have to do to earn the respect and status of a shaman is have a couple of piercings and wear a dress. Pat Califia wittily illustrated where this situation could lead to in *Skin Two* magazine:

> "Where's the altar? You never gave me any time to meditate before you tied me up. Can we do some tantric breathing and chanting together before we play? It's the Vernal Equinox you know. Those candles should be yellow and blue... If you're going to mummify me, you should put crystals over my chakras. And if you're going to hit me, I really want to dedicate my pain to Kali because she's my tutelary deity for this moon cycle. Are those plastic clips? I never let plastic touch my body. Wood absorbs aural vibrations so much better. Wait, let me look at that tattoo on your arm. Oh. It isn't very, well, tribal-looking, is it?"

It should never be forgotten that sexual magic is a *discipline,* and that anything that comes from exploring sexual magic techniques arises as a consequence of your discipline. It should be obvious that to get anywhere with sexual magic, you must become practiced with all the other aspects of magical work.

WHY DO SEXUAL MAGIC?

There is a common assumption in some quarters that all magicians indulge in unspeakable practices behind closed doors. But just because a belief is popular does not make it true, does it? When people start to voice an interest in sexual magic, I tend to ask them "why?" It's generally assumed that everyone is interested in sexual magic in the same way that it's generally assumed that everyone is extremely interested and curious about sex. While it follows that all sex-magicians must be magicians, it does not mean that all magicians have to be sex-magicians.

GENERAL POINTS TO CONSIDER

a) You are 'doing' sexual magic when you begin to understand and explore your own sexual feelings and behaviors from a magical perspective.

b) You are 'doing' sexual magic when you begin to untangle your attitudes, habits and projections about having sexual experiences with other people.

c) Sexual magic is just as concerned with learning how to 'let go' as it is with 'control'.

d) If you cannot practice sexual magic on your own, then you probably will be no good with a partner.

e) You are responsible for your own emotions.

f) Like any other type of magic, sexual magic can be at times inappropriate, boring, or not the best method of going about things.

g) Beware of Adepts or Witch-Queens who make offers out the blue to raise your kundalini, stoke up your chakras or blow your aura!

h) Never do sexual magic with anyone crazier than yourself.

IS SEXUAL MAGIC THE SAME AS TANTRA?

I deal with this question here as the two subjects are often confused. Tantra and Sexual Magic are *not* the same. Tantra itself is a vast subject, of which sex-magic practices constitute only a small part. Tantra can be translated as meaning 'tradition', 'to spread', and 'to weave', and it encompasses astrology, yoga, sorcery, alchemy, devotional worship, medicine, and the search for enlightenment. It is not a religion, though it does have religious elements, nor is it a way of thought; it is a way of action. Most importantly, to truly understand Tantra, you really need to seek initiation via a guru or your own practice.

Sexual Magic however, can be practiced without being rooted in one particular psycho-mythological belief system, requiring no more than a purposeful intent, skill in the techniques of magic, and a relaxed attitude to any possible experience or effect. The Chaos Magic approach has done much to disentangle practical magical techniques and procedures from the layers of ossified dogma that has built up around them. Most theories of 'occult sexuality' are no more than beliefs written as 'cosmic laws', the problems of which are discussed below.

BEWARE OF THEORIES WHICH SPIRITUALLY JUSTIFY PREJUDICES

Western approaches to magic retain the influence of the anti-sexual frothings of Theosophists, Christian Qabalah, and other such movements who proclaim themselves to be Right-Hand Path. Basically, the RHP syndrome seems to support the memes of servitude, karma, the division of mind, body, and spirit, and a rejection of sexuality, at some level. Witness the number of spiritual pronouncements which still circulate over the issues of doing sex-magick with someone who is not an established partner, or better yet, someone of

the same sex. Like any other arena of human exploration, occultism generates theories for explaining/under-
standing the myriad facets of human behavior. For
some, these theories are no more than signposts,
concepts to be discarded as the individual's knowledge
and insight develops. For others, the various theories
become dogmas—fixed beliefs which become firmly
entrenched in the individual's psyche as manifestations
of prejudice: attitudes perpetuated by ignorance.
Occult concepts of sexuality are no different to those
from any other angle of society—they can be used to
confirm prejudice, and elevate it to a 'spiritual' or
'traditional' plane of received wisdom. This becomes
clear when one sees occultists attempting to 'explain'
homosexuality. There is much invocation of chakra
imbalances, reverse kundalini, feminine souls in male
bodies, and so forth. The level of sophistication can
range from the simplistic "it's not natural" to extremely in-depth discussions about chakras, kundalini, and
damaged auras. Homosexuality and magick have, since
the beginning of the great occult revival of the last
century, been uneasy bedfellows, and there have been
few attempts to develop a gay approach to sex-magic
with any thoroughness, at least, that are available in
the public domain.

This is, in part, due to entrenched attitudes about
the 'magical' nature of homosexuality. A great deal of
occult theories currently in circulation were spawned in
the heyday of the Theosophical Society, for example
the identification of Left Hand Path of being all things
bad) and the Right Hand Path that of the 'good guys';
stems from the Theosophist's rejection of sexuality and
its active role in Tantra. When a leading member of the
Theosophist movement was implicated in a sex-scandal
involving pubescent boys, the resulting furor not only

damaged the Theosophical movement as a whole, but also gave rise to the rumors that there existed groups of 'Black Magicians' who obtained occult power by psychically vampirizing young boys. Such rumors were given a substantial boost by Dion Fortune, who alleged throughout the 1920s and 1930s that there was a conspiracy of male occultists who used 'homosexual techniques' to build up what she called 'dark astral power'. She also blamed the decline of the Greek and Roman empires on those cultures' relaxed attitude to homosexuality. Although she never named any of these 'black adepts', it is clear that she was probably referring to C. W. Leadbeater, and perhaps, also Aleister Crowley.

Crowley's attitude to homosexuality is ambivalent, to say the least. An active and enthusiastic bisexual, he had several male lovers, the most notable of which was the poet Victor Neuburg, his partner in a series of homosexual sex-magick operations known as The Paris Working, where Neuburg and Crowley performed a series of invocations using anal intercourse as the means of achieving gnosis. The results of this series of magical operations demonstrated to Crowley the power of sexual magick as a means of obtaining results, and he wrote magical papers on the value of VIII° (Autosexual), IX° (Heterosexual), and XI° (Homosexual) magick which were incorporated into his reworking of the Ordo Templis Orientis magical Order. Crowley also wrote a book of poems devoted to love between men, or more accurately, a man and a boy: *Bagh-I-Muttar: The Scented Garden of Abdullah the Satirist of Shiraz,* published in 1910. While a worthy addition to any collection of Crowley's work, the *Bagh-I-Muttar* is not a book of practical instruc-

162

tion. Exponents of Crowley's work such as Kenneth Grant and the late Israel Regardie have sought to 'excuse' his use of what Kenneth Grant calls 'the homosexual formula.'

Most modern textbooks of sexual magic either ignore male homosexuality, or take the position that the gender of partners makes no difference when it comes to "raising energy." They do, however, tend to stress the importance of sexual magick taking place between an established couple, and there are few (if any) references to the areas of gay sexual culture that 'straight' society finds so hard to handle—group sex, S & M or anonymous sex. Clearly, any writer able to overcome the general occult phobias over homosexuality (particularly male homosexuality—some occult sexual manuals say that Lesbianism is okay—after all, it's a turn-on, isn't it?) is valuable, compared to the 'blocked chakras' brigade, but by saying that 'the energies are essentially the same' and then going on to describe practices purely in heterosexual terms is missing out that there might possibly be something different about homosexual magic.

THE QUESTION OF POLARITY

I worked for a few years with an Alexandrian Coven, where polarity was an important issue. You know, all the stuff about male-female, positive-negative, bright-dark, low-high active-passive. The male-female bit was especially strong, and every Priestess had to have her Priest, and vice-versa. Men reflect the Horned One, and Women reflect the Triune Goddess and any suggestion that things could be otherwise, well it just wasn't done. So I learned to work with the Goddesses; being in a Wiccan coven meant having a 'magical partner' to work with—a Priestess. Slowly the subversive little thought crept in: "Why can't men work with the Goddesses directly, and women invoke the Horned (or any other God) upon themselves?" Okay, so I was naive at the time, but we tried it—no problems. By that time I'd read all the Jung I ever wanted to and was well into his concept of male and female natures within. The High Priestesses said that men needed to get in touch with their 'feminine' natures, so this was okay.

The concept of 'polarity', is in it's most simplistic form is the much-quoted idea of God and Goddess within the self. The *problem* of 'polarity' is when divinity is confused with conditioning and what is supposed to be 'masculine' and 'feminine' qualities. Thus we are told over and over that fire is *masculine* and water is *feminine*; that the capacity to display emotions and be intuitive are *feminine* and that intellectual analysis is *masculine*. Says who? Feminist critiques of conditioning make the point that we only know what masculinity and femininity are because they have been defined in specific ways. Working beyond these limitations is surely a primary task in the developmental process. So much of what passes for 'occult laws' is just a 'spiritualized' justification of social conditioning and prejudice. For Gay men, for example, polarity needn't be as simplistic as one partner assuming a feminine role— you can acknowledge the feminine and still stick your penis in another man. You can celebrate the masculine elements of psyche and still receive another man's cock into yourself. Goddesses and Gods are not subject to the same restrictions as humans—after all, what would be the point if they were? Imposing our own narrow limits upon them is to miss the point of the whole exercise of invoking them. I invoke upon myself to go beyond my present limitations—to join momentarily with something greater, or outside my ego. Sometimes my lover becomes to me a God, or a Goddess—regardless of their human gender or which of us is 'on the receiving end' of the other's attentions.

SEX & SELF-DISCOVERY—EGO MAGIC

Although we tend to regard our own sexual natures as private and intimate, our sexuality is subject to a great deal of interference and manipulation from external agencies. We are subjected to a media-carried imperative to be *good* at sex. Success is measured from the number of orgasms we can wring from our partners, or indeed, from the number of partners one has. Modern culture commodifies all aspects of sexual experience into forms which maintain alienation; contrasts such as Sentimental Romanticism and Pornography. More powerful and invasive than any medieval succubi are the neuroses and obsessions which become entangled with our experience of our own sexuality. Ego Magic, in this context, is concerned with untangling one's internal conversations, attitudes and projections concerning one's own sexuality. Much of what we call our sexuality is based on cultural conditioning although we do not (without practice) experience it as such.

This is a difficult undertaking at the best of times, and is a process that once well begun, never really stops fully. The key to unlocking this process is the understanding that it is difficult to modify any core aspect of one's persona unless the urge to change is stronger than the urge to remain static. This is particularly important when it comes to getting to grips with aspects of sexuality. Bear in mind that there is often a significant difference between the expectations we place upon ourselves (and others) and what we can actually do. In other words, there is a tendency to pay too much attention to what's in our heads rather than what's actually going on. This is not necessarily a bad thing, however. For example, while some people deny or refuse to admit that they sometimes have fantasies that their partner, during sex, is someone (or something) else, the same facility allows magicians to empty their awareness of everything but an image or sigil while being vigorously humped. Again, we must always recall that much of our sexuality is contextual and relational.

Ego Magic in relation to sexuality is not, as some magicians seem to think, merely a question of exploring forms of sexual expression which are unusual or repugnant. It is, after all, particularly easy to 'rationalize' experiences away, so that they do not threaten the mirror-reflection of self hood that one has. "Oh no dear, X and I didn't really have sex, it was a only a ritual." It is more a case of understanding and integrating internal conflicts—liberating 'demons' which we have kept bottled, for fear of how their eruption might overwhelm us. Slavery to either compulsion or repression are signs of unbalance to the effective magician.

It should also be pointed out that Ego magic is not only not easy, but is often unpleasant, as one begins to confront the aspects of one's experience which one would prefer not to. When experimenting with sexual boundaries, it is all too easy to quickly exchange one label for another. One heterosexual experience, does not after all, make you 'straight' just as one same-sex experience doesn't mean that you are gay, either. We are often too quick to label ourselves, particularly if we've just done something the night before which makes us question our identity in a different way. Partly this is due to a cultural tendency to polarise everything as one thing or another, and it is difficult sometimes, to relax and allow ourselves more fluidity of self-identification or expression, without anxiety.

It may sound like a cliché, but love begins at home. No amount of one-night stands will compensate for not feeling okay about yourself. Anyone who tells you that they are still looking for the 'right' partner so that they can practice sexual magic 'properly' still hasn't cottoned on to the basic fact that so-called sex-magic 'power' does not reside in other people, techniques, or in occult 'secret teachings.' All magical 'power' comes from within, and cultivating Self-Love is a first step to unleashing this power. Which is not to say that it is easy—it often isn't, and many people spend years struggling to like themselves. Self-Love requires that you accept yourself—warts and all, rather than trying to live up to a self-image which is unrealistic and unbalanced. Self-Love enables you to *relax* so that you are not continually flogging yourself with internal criticism, and, significantly, you do not feel an overwhelming need to have other people's approval. Self-Love changes the way we relate to others, so that we no longer use other people as props to support our fantasies, but begin to see them as independent agents. If you do not love yourself, then you will find it difficult to love other people—you will continually use others to prop up parts of your ego. Having made the point that Self-Love is necessary, the next step is to examine some pointers towards beginning the process of learning to live with yourself.

a) Honesty — The most effective magicians are those who can give an honest appraisal of themselves. This means recognizing your strengths and weaknesses, your successes and failures, doubts, fears and hopes, and being able to look at yourself without constantly

167

becoming depressed, or caught up in 'what if...but' projections. At times you may have to force yourself to admit that you have failures, as well as successes.

b) Live in the Present — You can't keep beating yourself up for all the mistakes you've ever made, yet it's really tempting to dwell on one's past errors, as by doing you can keep lying to yourself that you're a failure, everyone hates you etc. By the same token, you should stop trying to 'second-guess' every imminent future situation, particularly if you can only see one aspect of it. Also, it's too easy to get trapped by your past experiences so that you cannot possible envisage a situation where things could be different than what you're used to.

c) Trust Yourself — There is much mystical woffling about the development of the intuition, but it is important that you trust your own feelings about someone or something. We often 'go along' with other people for fear of upsetting them or 'losing' them, but in doing so, we devalue what we ourselves want, and subordinate it to what we think are the desires of others. If you've ever found yourself having sex with someone in order to 'keep the peace', then you should know what I mean here.

d) Check Your Expectations — It may be something of a cliché, but try asking yourself *if you are doing what's right for yourself.* We often do things because we have internalized someone else's expectations of what we 'should' or 'ought' to be doing. No matter what the source of the internalization—be it parents, peer group, friends etc., it still tends to boil down to the position that you're attempting to live by someone else's expectations, rather than your own. The inner conflict which this can produce can lead to much personal distress, through sustained guilt loops, unrealistic expectations which you'll *never* be able to match up to, and internalized 'voices' that seem to belong to someone else. Living for *yourself* is not easy, mind. It's much easier, or so it seems, to live your life according to other people's expectations and demands, than to find out what you actually desire.

EXO MAGIC

Exo Magic is 'Ego' Magic directed to understanding others—in terms of interpersonal transactions. This is particularly important, yet often ignored. It has been often said that the Western approach to magic is very 'head'-oriented, showing an obsession with symbols, numbers, abstract ideas and 'inner planes' which have little contact with the everyday world. Consequently you may occasionally meet self-professed magi who have plumbed the million spheres, spoken with archangels, received mystic wisdom from higher masters yet, are seemingly so exalted that they come across to us lowly beings as a complete klutz, unable to hold an everyday conversation. Small wonder that such sad types turn up at occult gatherings, where they hope that someone else will be so impressed by their 'spiritual power' that they will agree to take up the offered post of Scarlet Woman or Shakti.

SEX-DEMONS

One example of Exo Magic is working with Sexual Demons. By this I do not mean succubi or incubi, but the 'bundles' of behaviors, attitudes, emotions etc. which emerge during interpersonal transactions. I have labeled these as 'demons' as we often tend to experience them as beyond our control. Working with Sexual Demons is 'other-directed' as these 'demons' are not wholly intrapsychic structures, but depend on other peoples' behavior, and our own reaction to that behavior too. For example, if you become jealous due to the way that you perceive your partner behaving, then the ways in which your partner responds to your emotion will give further shape to the demon—it's not so much the case that being jealous is simply one person's problem—all parties concerned contribute to the shape of the sexual demon.

These structures become problematic when we become subject to them continuously, carrying them from one situation and relationship to the next, so that we are continually re-enacting the same cycle of behavior, with different partners. Eventually, it seems that the 'demon' becomes the organ-grinder and we are just the monkey dancing to its tune, unable to do anything about it or realize how we are perpetuating the cycle. Unlike traditional demons who can be looked up in grimoires, sex-demons often do not have a shape, sigil, name or character, yet they can come to exert tremendous power over us. They can be however, identified, bound and integrated, so that they work with us rather than against us.

It should be understood that *integrating* does not mean *suppressing*. For example, many people have problems acknowledging their own capacity for anger. Consequently, they tend to turn anger inwards, upon themselves, so that they suffer from frustration continually, allowing themselves only occasional 'fits' of anger which leave them surprised, guilty, and even less able to acknowledge this emotion. I once had a lover who was continually even-tempered and always had a kind word for everyone and everything, keeping himself under control—until he realized that he ground his teeth with suppressed rage in his sleep.

I find the magical injunction of "lust without result" is appropriate to this kind of emotional engineering. In this context, it is a reminder that our emotions are fluid and changeable, while we cling to the idea that we are a stable, hardly-changing personality. We often fear to let our emotions flow forth, as we fear the consequences—how others will see us, and by this time, we are already internalizing an idea of how we think others *do* see us. So much of these anxieties become wrapped up with the expression of sexual desire. A good example of this is chatting someone up. It's all too easy to get tongue-tied and nervous, especially if you're desperate or over-eager. But if you are relaxed in this kind of situation, you can afford to be playful. A person who is *playing* is free from attachment to the outcome of a situation (i.e., 'lust without result') and may thus take more risks than a person who walks in terror of losing his cool and looking stupid.

How, then, can we get to grips with these 'personal' demons?

1. Identify a 'demonized' habit or pattern: This requires some degree of insight into your own behavior. Observe yourself in social situations and find out how people are reacting to what you say and do. If, for example, you wonder why people continually give you the cold-shoulder despite your best efforts to impress, then you may well be following a pattern which has become so embedded in your psyche that you're not aware of it. Is it everyone else's fault that they can't see how splendid you are? This involves really *listening* to people, not just using them as sounding boards.

171

This, in itself, is difficult. Personal demons need to remain 'invisible' to survive, and, as they are usually related to core parts of your self-image, they will usually resist being identified, allowing you to justify your behavior (and self-image) so that you never have to really do something about it. Saying to people, "Oh, my Jealousy-demon slipped out just then" only reinforces your subservience to it.

2. Unpick the threads of the pattern: These 'demons' cannot be banished or integrated instantly—it takes time. Yes, you can try and enter into a dialogue with them, but doing the standard 'calling-up-into-a-triangle-and-threatening-with-a-sword' bit is insufficient here, because these 'entities' largely belong to the social world of interpersonal transactions. The best time to struggle with your 'Jealousy demon' is when you're on your own, and you suspect that your lover is off screwing someone else. When you are sitting alone, gut churning, imagining what they're doing, what you will do when they come back, what they will say, how you will react, it's easier to understand how the different components of the demon 'fit' together:

Component: Physical stress & negative self-statements: Intervention: Stop Thinking. Relaxation, Meditation, Pranayama etc. will stop the BodyMind feedback loop.

Component: Recycling the past, anticipating the future: Intervention: Relax 'into' your feeling while breathing deeply and stilling the internal dialogue. Let your bodily sensations fill your awareness until thoughts are stilled and you are only aware of an undefined sensation.

Component: Anticipated future situations which serve to reinforce your existing feelings: Intervention: Take

172

these fantasies to their logical (or illogical) conclusion. A lot of demonized patterns retain their power because they always lead to a situation which is *too terrible* to contemplate. Consequently, we never do confront (even in fantasy) that situation, and it remains an indistinct spectre. I recall once, in a bout of depression, thinking that I had screwed things up so badly there was nothing for it but to go away and start a new life somewhere else. So I began to get into this fantasy, which at first helped reinforce my self-pity, but eventually began to get so engrossing as I worked on the problem of becoming someone else, that I had exhausted my original self-doubt and was able to laugh at myself.

All magic is concerned with self-change and development. Sex-magic is particularly so concerned, as it requires that we understand our sexual natures, before we can effectively perform acts of "Love under Will." It may well take us the whole of our adult lives to fully comprehend and integrate our sexual feelings, as you cannot really expect to break all your sexual identifications and habits in one ritualized sexual act. But a sex-magic approach, above all, allows us to feel our sexuality to be sacred—in the sense that we should value, and take care of our sexuality—to treasure it's expressions and manifestations in all their forms.

APPENDIX ONE

THE LESSER BANISHING RITUAL
OF THE PENTAGRAM

The Qabalistic Cross
Facing east:
Touch your forehead and say Atoh
(aah—toh)
Touch your Heart and say Malkuth
(mal—kooth)
Touch your Right Shoulder and say Ve-Geburah
(veh —ghee—boo—rah)
Touch your Left Shoulder and say Ve-Gedulah
(veh—ghee—doo—lah)
Touch your Heart and say Le-Olam
(lee—oh —lum)
Point the symbolic dagger inward and say Amen
(aah—mayn).

Still facing east:

Trace the Banishing pentagram of Earth and vibrate
YHVH *(yoad—hay—vaahv—hay)*, as you thrust your
symbolic dagger into the heart of the pentagram.

With your arm still extended, turn to the South:
Trace the Banishing pentagram and vibrate the name
ADONAI (aah—doh—noy). [Remember to thrust the
symbolic dagger as you vibrate each God name].

With your arm still extended, turn to the West:
Trace the Banishing pentagram and vibrate the name
EHIEH (eh—hayh—yay).

With your arm still extended, turn to the North:
Trace the Banishing pentagram and vibrate the name
AGLA (ah—guh—lah).

With your arm still extended return to the East, completing the circle. Now Imagine yourself surrounded in a Flaming Circle of four Pentagrams.

Stand straight with your arms out forming the shape of a Cross: Say:

Before me *Raphael. (rah—fay—ale)*
Behind me *Gabriel. (gah—bree—ale)*
At my right shoulder, *Michael. (mee—khigh—ale)*
At my left shoulder, *Auriel. (oh—ree—ale)*

Then say:

Before me flames the Pentagram
Behind me shines the *six-rayed Star*.
Finish by repeating the Qabalistic Cross:
Touch your forehead and say *Atoh*
Touch your Heart and say *Malkuth*
Touch your Right Shoulder and say *Ve-Geburah*
Touch your Left Shoulder and say *Ve-Gedulah*
Touch your Heart and say *Le-Olam*
Point the symbolic dagger inward and say *Amen*.

APPENDIX TWO

THE MIDDLE PILLAR

Begin by imagining a *scintillating white light* a bit smaller than a basketball forming above the head and piercing the top of the skull. This is called the Kether point. Now vibrate the Divine Name *EHIEH (eh—hay—yay)* as the sphere of Light grows brighter and more energetic. Do this for five minutes.

As the force of this whirling ball of power becomes exceedingly real for you, allow the energy to descend slowly through the head. Allow it to rest in the throat, or Da'ath point. Imagine that the light has become a *lavender color*. Vibrate the Divine Name *YHVH ELOHIM (yeh—ho—vah ay—lo—heem)* until the energy becomes very real for you.

Bring the energy down through the chest until it rests at the Heart, or Tiphareth point. Vibrate the Divine Name *YHVH ELOAH VA DAATH (yeh—ho—vah el—oh—ah vah da—ahth)*. The color of the light should be *golden yellow*, growing brighter and clearer as you vibrate the Name.

Move the power through the diaphragm and abdominal region to the pelvis, the Yesod point, and vibrate the Divine Name *SHADDAI EL CHAI (shaa—dye el hi)* visualizing a sphere of *deep purple* light.

Finally, allow the energy to descend through the legs until it formulates at Malkuth, the feet. Vibrate the Divine Name *ADONAI HA-ARETZ (Ah—do—noy ha—ah—retz)* visualizing a *black* sphere.

Now, draw the energy up from Malkuth back to Kether, changing colors from Black, to Purple to Golden Yellow, to Lavender and finally back to White. When the light reaches Kether, meditate on the White brilliance of this region for a few moments.

Now begin the circulation of the White light.

Allow it to descend downward and outward via the *left* side of the body during every *exhalation*. When it reaches the left foot, transfer the energy over to the right foot and allow it to ascend the *right* side of the body on the *inhalation*. Continue this circulation at least ten times.

Now circulate the light down the *front* of the body on the *exhalation* and up the *back* of the body on the *inhalation*. Continue this at least ten times as well.

Finally, allow the White light to descend through the body from Kether to Malkuth on the *exhalation* and then draw the energy back up again to Kether on the *inhalation*. When the Light reaches the Crown at the end of the inhalation, allow it to discharge like water from a fountain. The fire and sparks of this scintillating fountain go up and out through the Crown and then descend down, encompassing the body on the exhalation.

APPENDIX THREE

THE MEDITATION OF THE SEER

"True Equilibrium is the basis of the Soul. If thou thyself has not a sure foundation, whereon wilt thou stand to direct the forces of nature.

"Know then that as Man is born into this world amidst the darkness of nature and the strife of contending forces, so must his first endeavour be to seek the Light through their reconciliation. Thus, thou who hast trial and trouble of this life, rejoice because of them, for in them is strength, and by their means is a pathway opened unto the Light Divine.

"How should it be otherwise, O man, whose life is but a day in Eternity, a drop in the Ocean of Time? How, if thy trials were not many, couldst thou purge thy soul from the dross of Earth?

"Thou therefore who desirest magical gifts, be sure that thy soul is firm and steadfast, for it is by flattering thy weakness that the Evil One will gain power of thee. Humble thyself before thy God, yet fear neither man nor spirit. Fear is failure and the forerunner of failure; and courage is the beginning of virtue. Therefore fear not the spirits, but be firm and courteous with them, for this too may lead thee into sin.

"A man is what he maketh himself within the limits fixed by his inherited destiny; he is a part of mankind. His actions affect not himself only, but also those with whom he is brought into contact.

"Neither worship nor neglect the physical body, which is thy temporary connection with the outer and material world. Therefore let thy mental equilibrium be above disturbances by material events. Restrain the animal passions and nourish the higher aspirations; the emotions are purified by intentional suffering.

"To obtain magical Power, learn to control thought. Admit only true ideas which are in harmony with the end desired, and not every stray and contradictory idea that presents itself. Fixed thought is a means to an end; therefore pay attention to the power of silent thought and meditation. The material act is but the outward expression of the thought, and it hath been said that 'the thought of foolishness is sin.' Thought therefore is the commencement of action, and if a chance thought can produce much effect, what cannot fixed thought do? Therefore, as has been already said, establish thyself firmly in the Equilibrium of Forces, in the center of the cross of the elements, that Cross from whose centre the creative word issued in the birth of the dawning universe.

"Be thou therefore prompt and active as the Sylphs, but avoid frivolity and caprice. Be energetic and strong like the Salamanders, but avoid irritability and ferocity. Be flexible and attentive to images like the Undines, but avoid idleness and changeability. Be laborious and patient like the Gnomes, but avoid grossness and avarice. So shalt thou gradually develop the powers of thy Soul and fit thyself to command the spirits of the elements."

APPENDIX FOUR

THE SIGNS OF THE GRADES

Shu

APPENDIX FIVE

BRIEF MEANINGS AND LOCATIONS
OF THE CHAKRAS

Sahasrara—Beyond the Chakra Centers. Above the head. Technically not a Chakra, although many call it one. Might be considered Kether, mixing with Ain Soph. This center is beyond language.

Ajna Chakra—#6 Located between the eyebrows. Relates to the region of the Mind-Ether. Sometimes called the third eye. The color is white. Beyond the notion of dimensions. The pure Mind. Divine Union of personal self with the Collective Self. Power to leave the body at will. The ability of the True Seer. This might be considered Chokmah and Binah, the first mating of Wisdom and Understanding.

Vishuddha Chakra—#5 Location, the throat region. Relates to Sound and Ether. Color is smoky purple. Power; freedom from possession by worldly activities, complete knowledge is obtained, of the past, present and future. Mandala is a circle. Animal is elephant. The organ is the mouth. Might be thought of as the "false" Sephirah Daath.

Anahata Chakra—#4 Location, the heart region. Relates to Air. The sense of touch and feelings. Color of the petals is blood red. Power of hearing Om with the inner ear. Power to protect and destroy the three worlds. Mandala is hexagram. Animal is the antelope. Organ is the penis. Tiphareth.

Manipura Chakra—#3 Location, the diaphragm-navel region. Relates to Fire. The Sense is sight and "emotions." The color of heavy rain clouds, dark blue. Power to create and destroy worlds and the wealth of personal knowledge. Mandala is a triangle. Animal is the ram. Organ is the anus. Can be associated with the Portal Grade, the passage between the Outer Order to the Inner Order.

Svadhisthana Chakra—#2 Located slightly above the genital region. The Sense is Taste. Color on the petals is vermilion. Relates to Water. Power of well reasoned discourse, or verse, imagination. Freedom from enemies. Mandala is the crescent. Animal is the alligator. Organ is the hand. Yesod.

Muladhara Chakra—#1 Location, the anal area. Relates to the earth. The sense is smell. Color is crimson. Power of Speech and eternal knowledge. Mandala is the square. The animal is the elephant. The organ is the feet. Malkuth.

APPENDIX SIX

THE BANISHING RITUAL OF THE HEXAGRAM

This ritual operates upon the Macrocosm in the same manner in which the Pentagram ritual operates upon the Microcosm.

1. Stand upright, feet together, left arm at side, right arm across body, holding the wand or other weapon upright in the median line. Then face East, and say:

2. "I.N.R.I.
Yod. Nun. Resh. Yod.
Virgo, Isis, Mighty Mother.
Scorpio, Apophis, Destroyer.
Sol, Osiris, Slain and Risen.
Isis, Apophis, Osiris, IAO."

3. Extend the arms in the form of a cross, and say: "The sign of Osiris Slain." (See illustration.)

4. Raise the right arm to point upwards, keeping the elbow square, and lower the left arm to point downwards, keeping the elbow square, while turning the head over the left shoulder looking down so that the eyes follow the left forearm, and say: "The sign of the Mourning of Isis" (See illustration.)

5. Raise the arms at an angle of sixty degrees to each other above the head, which is thrown back, and say: "The sign of Apophis & Typhon." (See illustration.)

6. Cross the arms on the breast, and bow the head, and say: The sign of Osiris Risen." (See illustration.)

7. Extend the arms again as in (3) and cross them again as in (6), saying:

"L.V.X. Lux, the Light of the Cross."

8. With the magical weapon trace the Hexagram of Fire in the East, saying: "ARARITA."

(This is a word created by the initials of a Hebrew sentence which means "One is His Beginning: One is His Individuality: His Permutation is One.") This hexagram consists of two equilateral triangles, both apices pointing upwards. Begin at the top of the upper triangle and trace it in an anti-clockwise direction. The top of the lower triangle should coincide with the central point of the upper triangle.

9. Turn to the South. Trace the Hexagram of Earth saying: "ARARITA."

This Hexagram has the apex of the lower triangle pointing downwards; it should be capable of inscription in a circle.

10. Turn to the West. Trace the Hexagram of Air saying: "ARARITA."

This hexagram is like that of Earth: but the bases of the triangles coincide, forming a diamond.

11. Turn to the North. Trace the Hexagram of Water saying: "ARARITA."

This hexagram has the lower triangle placed above the upper, so that their apices coincide.

12. Return to the East and repeat steps 1 through 7.

THE PSYCHOPATH'S BIBLE

Foreword by Nicholas Tharcher

Throughout time, psychopaths have gotten a bad rap. That is quite understandable since almost all of the world's religious and social philosophies have little use for the individual except as a tool to be placed in service to their notion of something else: "God," or the "collective," or the "higher good" or some other equally undefinable term. Here, finally, is a book which celebrates, encourages and educates the best part of ourselves — The Psychopath.

TO LIE IS HUMAN

Not Getting Caught Is Divine

Introduced by Robert Anton Wilson

Take a tour of the prison erected by the lies that society tells you…and the lies you tell yourself. Then, learn the tools to tunnel out…

"Is it possible to use language to undo the hallucinations created by language? …a few heroic efforts seem able to jolt readers awake… to transcend words."

— Robert Anton Wilson

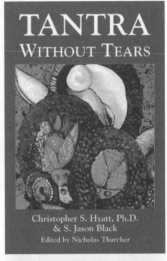

FROM CHRISTOPHER S. HYATT, Ph.D.

UNDOING YOURSELF WITH ENERGIZED MEDITATION

Introduced by Dr. Israel Regardie

Preface by Robert Anton Wilson

Innumerable practical techniques to transform your life, served up with a large dose of humor and the stick of the Zen Roshi.

Extensively illustrated.

"*Undoing Yourself* is the latest attempt by the Illuminati Conspiracy to reveal the hither-to hidden teachings." — Robert Anton Wilson

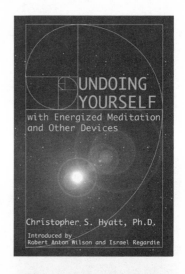

SECRETS OF WESTERN TANTRA

The Sexuality of the Middle Path

Introduced by J.M. Spiegelman, Ph.D.
Preface by Robert Anton Wilson

Dr. Hyatt reveals secret methods of enlightenment through transmutation of the *orgastic reflex*. Filled with explicit, practical techniques.

"The world's first scientific experimental yoga that does not expurgate the sensory-sensual-sexual aspects of the Great Work."

— Robert Anton Wilson

FROM CHRISTOPHER S. HYATT, Ph.D.

RADICAL UNDOING
The Complete Course for Undoing Yourself

For the first time on DVD, these effective and powerful Tantric methods help you to open your Chakras and release your Kundalini energy. With practice you will learn to harness this powerful sexual energy and experience *The Ultimate Orgasm*.

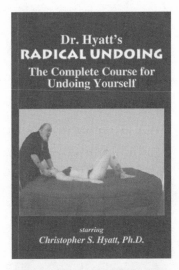

ENERGIZED HYPNOSIS
With Calvin Iwema, M.A.

Energized Hypnosis is a *breakthrough* program of DVDs, CDs, booklets and a non-book for gaining personal power, peace of mind and enlightenment. The techniques of **Energized Hypnosis** were developed many years ago by Dr. Christopher Hyatt and Dr. Israel Regardie, but have remained "in the closet"...until now.

THE *Original* FALCON PRESS

Invites You to Visit Our Website:
http://originalfalcon.com

At our website you can:

- Browse the online catalog of all of our great titles
- Find out what's available and what's out of stock
- Get special discounts
- Order our titles through our secure online server
- Find products not available anywhere else including:
    – One of a kind and limited availability products
    – Special packages
    – Special pricing
- Get free gifts
- Join our email list for advance notice of New Releases and Special Offers
- Find out about book signings and author events
- Send email to our authors
- Read excerpts of many of our titles
- Find links to our authors' websites
- Discover links to other weird and wonderful sites
- And much, much more

Get online today at http://originalfalcon.com